# Social Security
# After Fifty

**Recent Titles in**
**Studies in Social Welfare Policies and Programs**

Social Planning and Human Service Delivery in the Voluntary Sector
*Gary A. Tobin, editor*

Using Computers to Combat Welfare Fraud: The Operation and
Effectiveness of Wage Matching
*David Greenberg and Douglas Wolf*

Poverty and Public Policy: An Analysis of Federal Intervention Efforts
*Michael Morris and John B. Williamson*

Social Work: Search for Identity
*Leslie Leighninger*

# Social Security After Fifty

## SUCCESSES AND FAILURES

EDITED BY

## Edward D. Berkowitz

STUDIES IN SOCIAL WELFARE POLICIES AND
PROGRAMS, NUMBER 5

GREENWOOD PRESS
NEW YORK     WESTPORT, CONNECTICUT · LONDON

**Library of Congress Cataloging-in-Publication Data**

Social security after fifty.

(Studies in social welfare policies and programs,
ISSN 8755-5360 ; no. 5)
  Bibliography: p.
  Includes index.
  1. Social security—United States—History.
I. Berkowitz, Edward D.   II. Title: Social security
after 50.   III. Series.
HD7125.S5955   1987        368.4'3'00973        86-19383
ISBN 0-313-25542-3 (lib. bdg.: alk. paper)

Library of Congress Catalog Card Number: 86-19383
ISBN: 0-313-25542-3
ISSN: 8755-5360

First published in 1987

Greenwood Press, Inc.
88 Post Road West, Westport, Connecticut 06881

Printed in the United States of America

∞™

The paper used in this book complies with the
Permanent Paper Standard issued by the National
Information Standards Organization (Z39.48–1984).

10 9 8 7 6 5 4 3 2 1

# Contents

*Acknowledgments*                                                vii

1. Introduction: Social Security Celebrates
   an Anniversary
   *Edward D. Berkowitz*                                         3

2. Historical Perspectives on Old-Age Insurance:
   The State of the Art on the Art of the State
   *Mark H. Leff*                                                29

3. The First Advisory Council and the 1939
   Amendments
   *Edward D. Berkowitz*                                         55

4. Social Security and the Economists
   *Henry J. Aaron and Lawrence H. Thompson*                     79

5. The Plight of the Social Security Administration
   *Martha Derthick*                                             101

6. Social Security: A Source of Support for All Ages
   *W. Andrew Achenbaum*                                         119

7.  Social Security in 1995: The Future as a Reflection
    of the Past
    *Wilbur J. Cohen*                                      141

8.  A Reply to Wilbur J. Cohen
    *Robert J. Myers*                                      153

*Recommended Reading*                                      159

*Index*                                                    161

*About the Contributors*                                   167

# Acknowledgments

This book owes its origins to a conference held at George Washington University on March 22, 1986. The generosity and enthusiasm of Dean Clara Lovett made the conference possible. Professor William Johnson and Dean Henry Solomon added their enthusiastic support. I am grateful to all three.

The Prudential Foundation gave a timely donation that greatly aided the celebration of the fiftieth anniversary of social security. I would also like to acknowledge the help of Senator John Heinz and the staff of the Senate Committee on Aging. Not only did they participate in the fiftieth anniversary, they also gave permission to print some of their analysis in this volume.

Martha Derthick and Robert J. Myers helped immensely by providing comments on an earlier draft of chapter 1. They have my thanks. In writing that chapter and putting together the volume, I also benefited greatly from conversations with Wilbur Cohen and Blanche Coll.

Many members of the George Washington University community participated in the conference and in that way contributed to this volume. In particular, Professors William Griffith and Amitai Etzioni were generous with their time and ideas. Among the many others who put time and effort into the project were Robert

Forbes, Patricia Dilley, Ida Merriam, Burt Seidman, Paul Light, Eric Kingson and Forrest Chisman.

Closer to home, Carol Papish, Carolyn Hottle, and Todd Adkins eased the book into production. My thanks to each of them.

# Social Security
# After Fifty

# 1

# Introduction: Social Security Celebrates an Anniversary

EDWARD D. BERKOWITZ

On a hot and sticky summer day in Baltimore, Robert Ball turned to Wilbur Cohen and wished him a happy birthday. Ball's birthday wishes came during a quiet moment that followed the unveiling of a postage stamp in honor of the fiftieth anniversary of the Social Security Act. Ball spoke to Cohen in the history room of the Social Security Administration headquarters. Robert J. Myers stood near Cohen and Ball, enjoying the exhibits in the history room and appreciating the nostalgia of the occasion.

August 14, 1985 was not Cohen's birthday, nor could Ball be described as a man given to sentiment or to dwelling on past accomplishments. That made the moment all the more touching, a rare moment of self-congratulation among three men who personified the tradition of public service and stewardship that distinguished the social security program. As usual it was Ball and Cohen speaking to one another, with Myers affably hanging back: in the foreground two "high priests" of social security, to use Joseph Califano's expression, and in the background the program's former chief actuary.

Nor was the priestly designation inappropriate for this group. Each had taken a vow early in his career to protect and defend the program; each appreciated the program's mysteries and rituals.

Cohen characteristically turned Califano's epithet into a joke. The Cohens had always been priests, he said.

This band of three knew as much about the social security program as any three men or women alive. Even after fifty years, the program remained their program, and its birthdays were their birthdays.

Washingtonians tended to lump the three together, yet they were quite different from one another. Cohen and Myers went to work on the social security program in 1934. Cohen came as a research assistant to University of Wisconsin professor Edwin Witte, who served as executive secretary of the Committee on Economic Security, the group that helped to research and write the act signed by President Franklin Roosevelt on August 14, 1935. When the Social Security Board began operations later in 1935, Cohen became its first employee. He worked as a top-level assistant to Arthur Altmeyer, who ran the program from 1937 to 1953 and the person after whom the headquarters building in Baltimore was named. After Altmeyer's departure in 1953, Cohen remained at the Social Security Administration (SSA) until 1955, when he left SSA, never to return. His next government jobs were at the departmental, rather than the agency, level. In the Kennedy and Johnson years, he served as assistant secretary, under secretary, and ultimately secretary of the Department of Health, Education, and Welfare (HEW).

Myers's career followed a different course. He was an actuary with the Committee on Economic Security and then a member of the actuarial staff of the Social Security Board. Although W. Rulon Williamson served as the chief actuary, Myers soon acquired a reputation as a hard worker who produced reliable estimates on deadline. As Williamson wrote philosophical, even whimsical, memos on various aspects of economic security, Myers produced succinct actuarial estimates. In 1947 he acquired the title that matched his responsibilities and remained chief actuary until 1970, when he left on grounds of conscience. As he later told me in a personal letter, "the Nixon administration would not recognize, or at least do something about, the continuing expansionist philosophy within the SSA." Deeply involved in social security policy, Myers returned to SSA only once, a one-year stint as deputy commissioner during the Reagan administration, followed by another year as executive director of the National Commission on Social Security Reform.

Ball arrived later and only began to have real influence in the forties. He also stayed longer than the others in formal office. He was the only one of the big three to enter the agency from the field, but his talent soon brought him into central administration. Although, like Myers, his job titles seldom described his real responsibilities, he ultimately became commissioner in 1962 and remained for eleven years.

Something of the differences among Ball, Cohen, and Myers can be gleaned from the books that they found time to write during their various consulting and academic stints. In the fifties, Cohen went to the University of Michigan and wrote a book called *Retirement Policies Under Social Security*. This historical and legislative book exemplified the institutional analysis that Cohen had learned from Professor Witte at Wisconsin. Myers, who became a professor at Temple University after leaving government service in 1970, produced a book that might be described as the "data bible" of social security: crammed with details, with numbers, and with a sense of the technical complexity of social security. Ball, who characteristically remained in Washington rather than take an academic job elsewhere (Cohen, by way of contrast, worked in Ann Arbor and Austin, Texas but never sold his house in suburban Washington), wrote a book on social security that took the form of a Socratic dialogue. It attempted to explain in relatively simple language how social security worked and what policy problems it faced; issued by an academic publisher, it was nonetheless quite direct, with neither the numerical detail of Myers nor the historical detail of Cohen.[1]

These differences in print extended to the public impressions the three men made. Cohen was an extraordinarily unpretentious man, particularly when judged by Washington standards. He returned all of his phone calls unless he was ill or otherwise inconvenienced; he devoted as much attention to graduate students as to university presidents. A short, stocky, and balding man, he looked quite ordinary, a fact that put people at ease. He retained some of the eagerness, the desire to please, that had made him Edwin Witte's favorite student. Sometimes, for example, he erupted with enthusiasm and began to drive his points home by gesticulating forcefully with his finger. He was so open in his personal dealings and about his feelings that people liked him, felt comfortable with him, and seldom stood on ceremony with him. Secretary Cohen quickly gave way to Wilbur.

Of the three, Cohen came closest to representing the original vision of social security as a comprehensive program that covered people of all ages. To borrow W. Andrew Achenbaum's phrase from chapter 6, this 1935 vision was "transgenerational." In the legislative deliberations, the welfare system and unemployment compensation attracted far more attention than did old-age insurance. Only one aspect of these programs, aid to the elderly, concerned the elderly; the rest focused on the working-age population (unemployment insurance) and children (aid to dependent children). The act, which is best regarded as an omnibus piece of legislation that brought together nearly all existing federal social welfare programs, also contained such features as grants to the states for public health, crippled children, vocational rehabilitation, and infant and maternal health. None of these supplementary programs centered on the elderly. Only in the forties and fifties did old-age insurance emerge as the most important economic security program, important enough to monopolize the term "social security."

Something of the confusion that such a large piece of legislation engendered was captured by the young Wilbur Cohen just after the act became law. "The congressmen have a very confused idea what this whole program is about," Cohen wrote. "They mix up old-age assistance with old-age benefits, and they mix up old-age insurance with unemployment insurance."[2]

Cohen, a product of the Wisconsin institutional tradition, had an interest in a wide range of social programs, not just old-age insurance, and he thought deeply about how programs related to one another. As Cohen's essay in this volume demonstrates, he became an expert in social policy, rather than social security policy. The pattern of his career reinforced the range of his interests. He worked as Arthur Altmeyer's assistant at a time when Altmeyer administered welfare programs, unemployment compensation, and old-age and survivors insurance. Then, when he left SSA and came to academia and later to HEW, his interests broadened even more to include such topics as education and drug regulation. He helped to develop mental retardation legislation in the Kennedy administration, for example, and as late as 1978, he served on the National Commission on Unemployment Compensation.

Robert Ball was a far more enigmatic man than Wilbur Cohen. Not to do him a disservice, he looked unremarkable, the sort of man who would be difficult to categorize on the basis of his appearance. He spoke with little of Cohen's passion, yet he radiated an extraordinary sense of competence and authority. In congressional testimony, for example, he appeared able to anticipate the direction that the questions might take. That ability exemplified his remarkable sense of strategy. Although Ball had a strong sense of social duty, he was quintessentially a man of Washington, a man who felt comfortable in the maze of congressional committees and of Democratic party politics. Cohen wore his sentiments on his sleeve; Ball seldom revealed his ultimate objectives.

If Cohen thought about social policy, Ball concentrated on social security. He focused on old-age, survivors, and disability insurance, and medicare. Welfare, although well within his field of expertise, concerned him less. Reflecting his priorities, he had helped to institutionalize the separation between welfare and social insurance. When he became commissioner of the Social Security Administration in 1962, he played a role in the creation of the Welfare Administration, a new independent agency within HEW (1963). This desire to isolate social security proved quite astute as the Welfare Administration and its bureaucratic successors became conspicuous platforms for bureaucratic failure. Social workers and rehabilitators threw one strategy after another at the "welfare problem" without apparent success; often they threw away their own careers in the effort. Through the turmoil of the sixties, by way of contrast, the SSA rode high, wide, and handsome. Ball presided over the program's successful coming of age. He proved, if such a proof were needed, that do-gooders need not be softheaded.

At the fiftieth anniversary ceremony, Ball drew the loudest and most sustained round of applause. When the ceremonies were over, an employee of SSA approached him and said, "I don't have to tell you that things went to hell around here after you left." That was at least partially true. After Ball left, it became more difficult for the agency to specialize in social insurance to the exclusion of welfare. In 1972, while Ball was still commissioner, SSA was given responsibility for a federally administered welfare program called Supplemental Security Income. Martha Derthick's essay in this volume discusses the less than smooth implementation of this program that occurred after Ball left. Problems also arose with the administration of the black lung program in aid of handicapped coal miners. In retrospect, then, Ball's tenure came to be regarded as a golden age of social security, and his departure seemed to mark the dividing line between an era when the agency was special and an era in which social security encountered the same problems as many other government agencies.

Robert J. Myers sat with the current social security actuaries at the Baltimore ceremony. He belonged there. Of the three social security insiders, Myers was the most specialized: the only one with the technical training that enabled him to make projections about the long-run costs of the program. He also knew an extraordinary amount about how the program worked at the operational level; he kept up with such things as the Program Operating Manual System, a continuing series of instructions that the central agency sent to the field offices on how to administer the program. As Robert Ball said, Myers was the only one of the three who still knew how to compute a benefit. Indeed, Myers delighted in the technical nooks and crannies of the program and could discuss, for example, the changes in the calculations of the "primary insurance amount" that occurred in 1967 (when the formula, effective February 1968, was changed to the following: 71.16 percent of the first $110 of average monthly wages plus 25.88 percent of the next $290 plus 24.18 percent of the next $150 plus 28.43 percent of the next $100) along with other changes in the program.[3]

Myers looked dignified, professorial. As he aged, his hair became white, and he wore it rather long so that it curled in the back. The thin frames of his not-quite wire rim glasses added to the image as did his tall, thin body.

Myers was a stickler for detail and intellectual rigor. His exacting marginal comments on draft papers and memos, his letters to the editors of newspapers and journals correcting articles were legendary. His intellectual habits were those of an actuary. Therefore, he tended to judge the desirability of a program or piece of legislation in insurance terms and not just on its social desirability.

It mattered vitally whether a particular risk, such as disability, was "insurable." More than his colleagues, Myers worried about such things as the "moral hazard problem," whether, for example, one could separate people who were genuinely disabled from those who merely claimed to be disabled. Such concerns made him far more cautious about the expansion of social security than were Ball or Cohen. Of the three, Myers was politically the most conservative and the most wary of overstepping the instructions of particular presidential administrations. It was no accident that Myers left SSA during the Nixon administration.

It was also no accident that he stayed only a short while in the Reagan administration. It was one thing for Reagan to endorse changes in the rules of the disability program so that people qualified only on the basis of medical factors; that made sense from an insurance point of view. It was quite another thing for Reagan to support the notion that social security could be replaced by private savings and to undermine the public's confidence in social security.

Myers, for all his passion for detail, maintained a strong loyalty to the social security program and took great pride in the program's accomplishments. It did not worry him, for example, that as social security approached its fiftieth anniversary, it had paid $1,800 billion in benefits to 115 million people or that the average benefits for an aged couple reached $776 a month.[4] He was also not without his own sense of social service. Like Cohen, Myers belonged for many years to Group Health Association, a Washington, D.C. health care cooperative. At one point, he served on its board of trustees.

In thinking about himself and his colleagues, Cohen regarded their talents as complementary and leading to a natural division of labor. Cohen worked on social policy, broadly defined, and on public education concerning social security. Ball interpreted the social security program to Congress and made sure of its political survival. Myers supplied the technical know-how and integrity that were vital to a program that made decisions affecting the future on the basis of current information.

During the anniversary year, Cohen, Ball, and Myers crisscrossed the nation, recounting social security's accomplishments and impressing audiences with the need for its survival. Myers and

Cohen did the bulk of the travelling, as Ball was more often needed in Washington. In March, for example, the two flew to Albuquerque to attend a special colloquium. There they talked to reporters, patiently explaining that social security was in good fiscal health, ready to begin its second half-century. Over and over, they made the point that people should have faith in social security. The mistrust of government's competence and ability to make good on its promises was unfounded. As a feisty Eveline Burns, a longtime follower of social security and a member of the Committee on Economic Security staff in 1934, put it in Albuquerque during her last public appearance, "One of the worst things being done is the effort to destroy people's faith in the functions and intentions of the government. As long as we do that, we are going to do a lot of other stupid things."[5]

When Myers made one of his frequent appearances on the fiftieth anniversary circuit, he brought a report card with him. He graded social security in such areas as economic security and administration. He supplemented letter grades with written comments. On financial soundness, for example, Myers wrote, "Trust fund very likely secure for at least 75 years." He gave social security an A in this area; the program earned A's in all areas, with the significant exception of public confidence, which Myers gave a C, writing about the public's "misplaced anxiety."[6]

Myers did what he could to dispel this anxiety, as did Cohen and Ball. As social security spokesman James Brown, who like most social security employees had a long record of service with the agency, put it, "We are using the 50th anniversary of social security to shore up confidence in social security."[7]

Why did the public need to be persuaded to support social security when so many people had benefited from this seemingly reliable program? Coloring everything was the fact that the program came close to going bankrupt twice in a very short period of time. That made people uneasy. Cohen, Ball, and Myers, older men defending one of the federal government's oldest social welfare programs, called for the assistance of younger people to defend the program but found few willing to take up the cause. Among those who cared about social security, this problem of how to replace the generation of great leaders was a very real one. Arthur Altmeyer had given way to Robert Ball, but no one had ever really taken over from Ball. Edwin Witte produced Wilbur Cohen, but Cohen had not yet produced a similar protégé. And Robert Myers appeared beyond replacement. No one, it seemed, had the intelligence and political sense of Ball, the social vision of Wilbur Cohen, or the technical competence of Robert Myers.

There were, of course, good reasons for those things. In the modern era, with the explosion of government responsibilities, just keeping up in one area of social policy was a full-time undertaking: no more generalists like Cohen or Witte. Ball was sustained in his leadership role by a sense of mission and by legislative victories; present conditions were much more wearing, more conducive to burning out executives.

Neither the lack of legislative victories nor the age of the social security leaders explained the lack of public confidence. What about Ronald Reagan? Although old, Reagan managed to rally people to his cause in part because he told people what they wanted to hear. Perhaps people did not want to listen to the Ball-Cohen-Myers message; perhaps they simply distrusted the public social welfare programs.

Ronald Reagan himself did little to restore public confidence in social welfare programs. During the fiftieth anniversary, for example, the administration kept a low profile. The president did issue a reassuring statement to the effect that "social security has proven to be one of the most successful and popular [federal] programs." In meetings that preceded the fiftieth anniversary, however, John Svahn, who advised Reagan on domestic policy and served as his first commissioner of social security, remarked that perhaps the administration could celebrate the anniversary in a way that emphasized the private sector. Administration planners of the event at the Social Security Administration in Baltimore (there was no comparable event in Washington) made sure that Cohen was not allowed to give a formal speech. Instead, that honor fell to Secretary of Health and Human Services Margaret Heckler who was herself under fire for being too liberal and was soon dispatched to Dublin. Cohen at least sat on stage because of his work with the Postal Service as a member of the stamp selection committee. Ball sat in the audience, out of harm's way.

The Reagan attitude toward social welfare programs reflected the attitude of many in American society. The era belonged to

Charles Murray, who wrote a popular book on *Losing Ground* in social policy, as much as to Wilbur Cohen or Robert Ball. One of Murray's easiest targets was Aid to Families with Dependent Children (AFDC), one of the original programs in the Social Security Act. In 1935, it seemed beyond reproach. As the staff of the Committee on Economic Security explained, its purpose was to "prevent the disruption of families on the ground of poverty alone and to enable the mother to stay at home and devote herself to housekeeping and the care of her children, releasing her from the inadequacies of the old type of poor relief and the uncertainties of private charity."[8] In the eighties, the objectives of this program had become much more tangled. Murray expressed the repressed thoughts of many when he posed a hypothetical example of a world without welfare. "Suppose," he said, "I am a woman age 18 and I have a boyfriend and I know that there is absolutely nothing out there if I get pregnant and have a baby, except that boyfriend to support me and myself getting a job." Then, "my behavior is going to change," Murray said, implying that the existence of welfare payments for having children encouraged promiscuity, particularly among poor blacks.[9]

Defenders of social security would be quick to point out the limitations of Murray's observations: more whites than blacks receive welfare, and most welfare recipients are children who should not be punished for the actions of their parents. But the defenders of social security would also point out that Murray was not talking about social security; he was writing about welfare, which is far from the same thing. As Senator Proxmire said on the floor of the Senate, social security is "not welfare": "Too many people confuse it, unfortunately, with some kind of means test or some kind of welfare."[10] Yet whether or not the confusion was warranted, it remained in the public mind and undermined confidence.

If any single group needed their confidence in social security bolstered, it was the young. Among members of the baby boom generation, the largest single age group in the population, it became commonplace to hear discussions on financial planning in which social security was "zeroed out," assumed not to exist by the time the person reached retirement. Viewed in this manner, social security became an extraordinary burden, something for which people paid without getting anything in return. Even a respectful fiftieth anniversary story in the *New York Times* led with a mention of the "erosion of confidence in social security." The story cited an American Association of Retired Persons poll that showed that among people 25 to 34 years old—baby boomers— two thirds said they were "not too confident" or "not all that confident" in the system. Cohen, with characteristic honesty, said that he was most worried about "the failure of young people to understand the value of social security."[11]

As Cohen realized, many factors mitigated against this under- standing on the part of the young. Although some were having children and assuming heavy financial responsibilities, some still regarded themselves as beyond demography, immortal. Such peo- ple hardly troubled themselves with such contingencies as death and disability and therefore failed to see the value of the disability and survivors protection that social security provided. As befitted a generation that grew up in the midst of a liability crisis, the baby boomers also saw alternatives to social security in the form of litigation. If disability and death were in some sense preventable, then, more often than not, someone was at fault. Perhaps a doctor failed to perform his duty properly or perhaps a person drove carelessly. Such perceptions led to lawsuits, which brought far greater rates of return than social security offered and made social security the inferior, the alternative to welfare.

As illustrated by their penchant for litigation, the baby boomers demanded an instant gratification that was antithetical to social security. The members of the baby boom grew up in a time of soaring inflation, and that also tended to temper their zeal for long-term investment; chronic inflation implied that spending rather than saving was rational. It took something like individual retirement accounts (IRAs) to induce this generation to save. IRAs offered tax advantages in the short run and promised, with little apparent sacrifice or risk, high rates of return. IRAs saved a person money now and made him rich later. Social security, with its notion of banding together as a nation to reduce economic insecurity, cost money in the short run and was uncertain in the long run.

The feeling of uncertainty among the young explained their pen- chant for instant gratification and helped to explain their disen- chantment with social security. Much of the baby boom experience reflected opportunity gone sour. Many had been teenagers in the prosperous sixties only to see the jobs disappear in the seventies. It was not implausible that something similar might happen to social security: the gravy train stopping with the baby boomer's parents.

In this way, young people learned to distrust social security and explored private-sector alternatives. Policymakers in Washington began to hear about generational inequity. The elderly, it seemed, were extraordinarily successful in taking money from the young through such transfer programs as social security. As one consequence, poverty rates among the old were lower than poverty rates among children. Some politicians began to see possibilities in harnessing the votes of the baby boom generation. Toward this end, Governor Lamm of Colorado said that "America's elderly have become an intolerable burden on the economic system and the younger generation's future."[12] The young, the governor implied, needed to look out for their interests.

Not only a present sense of grievance among the young but future demographic patterns served to heighten the problem. In 2030, for example, the population over 65 will reach 65 million (compared with 29 million today), and the life expectancy of people over 65 will probably be significantly greater than at present.[13] Since social security basically depended on pay-as-you-go financing and since the relatively few members of the baby bust would have to pay the pensions of the relatively large baby boom, how would social security possibly be financed? If the system will go bankrupt in the twenty-first century, why should the baby boom waste its resources financing the retirement of present retirees?

The cynicism of the young toward social security was also fueled by their feelings toward politicians. Policymakers came up with the money to save the social security system from going bankrupt in 1983 through a brilliantly conceived political compromise. As Myers and others noted, this compromise will in all likelihood make the social security system solvent until 2050. Yet the solvency, as Henry Aaron and Lawrence Thompson point out in chapter 4, depends on building up a surplus in the trust fund through the year 2030 that will be used to fund the retirement of the baby boom. Some wondered if the policymaking system would allow such a surplus to develop; a large surplus in the trust fund represents a great temptation. In other words, the near-term solvency of the program is assured and today's elderly can rest easy. The long-run solvency of the program depends on good planning and on fiscal restraint. Furthermore, nothing can really be done to improve the situation now. As David Stockman noted, "I'm not going to spend a lot of political capital solving some other guy's problem in 2010."[14] Nor would any politician.

The entire discussion grated against the sensibilities of Cohen, Ball, and Myers as they travelled on the fiftieth anniversary circuit. Americans simply could not be convinced of social security's solvency; they seemed to believe that they were living in an atomized world in which generations were distinct from one another. The abstraction called the "old" too seldom materialized in their minds as their grandparents, their parents, and ultimately themselves. They failed to see their social security life insurance and disability insurance policies as the valuable assets that they in fact are.

So, as America celebrated the fiftieth anniversary of social security, social security often seemed more a fragile institution from the past than a vital part of the future. Those Americans who wanted to wallow in good, clean nostalgia chose to celebrate the fortieth anniversary of the battles and conclusion of World War II. A year earlier, Ronald Reagan had made a speech on the shores of Normandy that later appeared as an advertisement in his 1984 campaign; when he chose to look backwards, as he so often did, he liked his victories pure and his lessons simple. We won World War II; whether Dr. New Deal cured economic insecurity was still in doubt.

## ENTER THE ACADEMICS

As Cohen, Ball, and Myers were painfully aware, the outlook for social security had been quite different in 1960, during the last major social security anniversary. In that year, social security received bipartisan congratulations, and few saw major problems on the horizon. To celebrate, the Social Security Administration rounded up some centenarians who were receiving social security benefits; in that way the agency established links between the program and the major events of American history. Former slaves, descendants of families which had arrived on the Mayflower, and stage coach drivers all were to be found among social security

beneficiaries. When the day of the anniversary dawned, Tom
Wicker filed a story in which he called social security a "permanent
part of American life." The only real question, according to
Wicker, was how to expand social security.[15]

It turned out that the expansion of social security was very much
on John F. Kennedy's mind as he travelled to Hyde Park on August
14, 1960. There he joined thousands of people at Franklin D.
Roosevelt's grave and gave a strong campaign speech on the subjects of social security and health insurance. Kennedy used the
occasion to end a long feud with Eleanor Roosevelt. Social security
brought people together.[16]

Twenty-five years later, both Kennedy and Mrs. Roosevelt were
dead, and the Roosevelt children were aging. President Reagan
felt no compulsion to worship at FDR's grave. This time Governor
Mario Cuomo made the pilgrimage to Hyde Park. Unlike Kennedy
he was not his party's nominee or titular head; he represented the
party's liberal wing. The crowds for Cuomo were smaller than they
were for Kennedy, the subject of social security less a sure-fire
draw, the personal bonds that people felt to President Roosevelt
less compelling. Unlike Tom Wicker, Robert Pear did not file a
story about social security as a permanent part of American life.

Between 1960 and 1985 something paradoxical happened to the
subject of social security. As social security became more difficult
for Myers and Cohen and Ball to defend (if not less worthy of
defense) and as social security itself became a less popular institution, its popularity in academia and in think tanks broadened.
Bad news for the insiders had a salutary effect on the outsiders.

To use a favorite adjective among academics, social security had
grown "interesting" to political scientists, economists, and historians. In the field of political science, for example, social security
commanded relatively little attention in 1960. It was not the stuff
of elections, at least since 1940. It offered little of the congressional
trade-offs and log rolling that characterized a program like public
works. It appeared to be a program devoted to routine procedures
and incremental change, something like a postal service that delivered the letters on time.

By 1985 social security's placid image among political scientists
had changed. First, as Martha Derthick noted, the very absence
of conflict in social security was interesting. Her observation ar-

rived just in time to make social security a case study for critiques of pluralism and interest group liberalism and for theories that explained how the state could be an agent in its own expansion. And just when people began to comprehend social security as embodying a new type of politics, traditional partisan politics broke out. As the program reached its anniversary, political scientists began to record epochal battles over social security financing and over removing people from the disability rolls. In addition, important questions about administration arose, such as those posed by Martha Derthick in chapter 5.[17]

If social security had little popularity among political scientists in 1960, it had less among economists. The program embodied an intellectual tradition of institutional economics that was rapidly dying in the profession. Wilbur Cohen called Edwin Witte "the last of the eminent pre–World War II economists who were not econometricians but rather blended social history with social policy in an effort to obtain social reform."[18] As Cohen implied, institutional economics had become passé because economists had discovered the value of quantitative analysis in formulating problems and reaching solutions.

Economics as a discipline grew closer to decision-making theory, but in social security so many of the decisions had already been made. Scholarly writing about social security had the task of describing the program, which, because the program was so complicated, became an end in itself. Economists stayed away or wrote laudatory pieces on how effectively the program worked. In 1972 their services became even less in demand when Congress put automatic cost of living adjustments into the program.

Then, as in political science, things changed. Paradoxically, indexing made the program heavily dependent on economic forecasting, particularly when wages, prices, and unemployment rates began to deviate from past patterns. Furthermore, the erratic behavior of the economy raised policy questions in social security of interest to economists. Finally, the very growth of the program made it interesting to economists. Clearly, such a large program affecting so much of the labor force played a role in such economic matters as the labor supply, the labor force participation rate, and the savings rate. Henry Aaron and Lawrence Thompson discuss these matters fully in chapter 4.

In the years between 1960 and 1985, as well, historians began to give social security a history. Because this history sets the stage for the chapters that follow, it might be worthwhile to consider it in some detail here. In part, historians followed the lead of political scientists like Martha Derthick and Stephen Skowronek and noticed the differences between social security and other social welfare programs. Unlike welfare, for example, social security did not depend upon local or congressional gatekeepers, and that made it a radically different program from previous efforts at social welfare. Furthermore, it offered its beneficiaries money, rather than services, and that separated it from the federal social welfare programs of the twenties such as infant and maternal health or vocational rehabilitation. Finally, as the program matured, it developed the brilliant notion of an implied contract between the government and its citizens. That, in turn, helped to remove it from the partisan control and congressional tampering that had hampered so many efforts at American state-building. If social security were regarded as an ironclad contract to nearly everyone (as opposed to just veterans or blacks or women), then Congress could not indulge in its usual bargaining and trade-offs, and the program would have to be staffed with people competent enough to deliver the goods. It could not be manned by the political parties in the partisan style of a nineteenth-century customs house or post office.[19]

It was not enough, of course, for social security to include the idea of an implied contract. Such a notion also applied to earlier social insurance programs such as workers' compensation. Yet workers' compensation often degenerated into partisan fights over benefit levels and was not characterized by highly professional administration. The difference between the two programs appeared to lie in the fact that workers' compensation offered current protection, supplied by private insurance companies, against the risk of industrial accidents. Old-age insurance represented protection against a future risk administered by the federal government. As a result of the program's future orientation, it handcuffed members of Congress more than workers' compensation tied the hands of state legislators. In addition, the presence of federal rather than private administrators simplified the pattern of interest group politics with which legislators had to contend. The result was a less contentious program.

Even as historians drew these flattering comparisons, historians were aware that social security struggled over the course of many years to achieve its security and stature, a point developed by Mark Leff in chapter 2. Critical steps along the way included the 1939 amendments, the subject of chapter 3, and the 1950 amendments, described below.

As a result of the 1950 amendments broadening coverage and raising benefit levels, social security vanquished its rivals among social welfare programs. When Senator Moynihan discussed the history of the program on the floor of the Senate in 1985, he correctly called it a response to the problems of urban America. It represented a strain of reform that policymakers had used to cure the ills of industrial society. In this vein, Tom Wicker's 1960 story on social security portrayed it as a "complete break with the iron philosophy of the industrial revolution."[20] In keeping with this tradition, the original act excluded all but industrial and commercial workers from coverage.

The consequences were many. For one thing, financing schemes that depended on general revenues became suspect. It would be difficult to ask a farmer to pay taxes to support the pension of a retired steelworker and not ask the steelworker to do the same for a retired farmer. That, in turn, complicated the politics of social security since the congressman in an agriculture district could not be expected enthusiastically to support social security. Wilbur Cohen, in a 1937 memo on the exclusion of the self-employed from social security, worried that, "If we are going to tax this group in order to pay the subsidy necessary but not include this group in the benefits, I think we are going to find that we will have a very difficult problem on our hands. I think that the problem of providing a subsidy from the general revenue is likely to have a lot of dynamite in it. . . . "[21] For another thing, the exclusion of all but industrial and commercial workers meant that the only social welfare programs with universal coverage were welfare programs with means tests, such as aid to the elderly. Universal coverage (at least for the very poor) under state welfare programs heightened the demand for broader welfare benefits and made the number of potential welfare recipients much larger than potential social se-curity beneficiaries. That in turn undermined support for social security.

When the 1950 amendments were debated in the House of Rep-resentatives, Thomas Kean of New Jersey said, "We are at the crossroads. The old-age assistance program has grown by leaps and bounds. More than twice as many of our older citizens are receiving old-age assistance as are receiving payments under OASI." Representative Doughton of North Carolina noted that the "decision is whether the insurance program of the social se-curity system can be strengthened and reinforced against the as-saults of general old age pensions. . . . "[22]

Three factors helped to break the impasse on social security coverage that had prevailed in the forties. One concerned public finance. Agricultural states had a higher welfare rate among the elderly than did industrial states. That meant that taxpayers in those relatively poor states had to support a substantial number of the elderly, because states contributed part of the funds needed to pay welfare. Extending coverage to agricultural workers would mean that they could receive social security rather than welfare and that part of the tax burden would be shifted from the state to the federal government.

A second factor involved what political scientist Stephen Skow-ronek calls administrative capacity. An advisory council convened in 1947 and 1948, upon the heels of a 1946 congressional report that called "extension of coverage" the most "pressing" need in social security, took as its goal "to prevent dependency through social insurance and thus greatly reduce the need for assistance." This council noted that an earlier advisory council had recom-mended an extension of coverage but could not figure out a way of collecting contributions from farmers, the self-employed, and others. In the forties, however, the extension of the income tax changed the situation. As the advisory council noted, "The fact that almost all full time and a large proportion of part-time self-employed persons have for the last few years been required to file income-tax returns has radically altered the outlook for extending coverage to this group. It has been demonstrated that income reports can be obtained from the great majority of the self-em-ployed." In the twenties, when the Lynds studied conditions in

Muncie, Indiana, they found that 12 to 15 percent of the wage earners reported incomes large enough to make filing federal income tax necessary. World War II helped to change that. Since the technology of tax collection had improved, the administrative problems of extending social security coverage were considerably less.[23]

A third factor in extending coverage under social security related to politics and ideology. Social security occupied the middle of the road between the conservative and liberal alternatives that were offered. These alternatives included a Republican plan sponsored by Representative Curtis of Nebraska that would have created "a universal flat pension system which may be financed on a strictly pay-as-you-go basis."[24] Such a plan had the advantages of universal coverage, a smaller bureaucracy, and better control over costs from year to year. At the liberal end of the spectrum, proponents of the Townsend bill offered a similar plan except with higher benefits. Social security could therefore be portrayed as the rational alternative that rewarded work and offered workers more security in the long run, since benefits under the other plans could be summarily cut in any one year.

By broadening coverage to include farm and domestic workers, as well as some of the professional self-employed, and by raising benefits substantially, the 1950 amendments helped to turn back the threat posed by existing public welfare programs and by the liberal and conservative alternatives. Because of these amendments, for example, nearly 100,000 people who had been on welfare became eligible for social security, and by the beginning of 1951 the number of people on social security surpassed the number of people on welfare.[25]

Even more important, the 1950 amendments helped to break the mold of American social welfare programs and to launch social security into the years of its greatest success. No longer was social insurance reserved for urban and industrial America. Now all of America participated. Unlike the earlier programs of the progressive era and the New Deal, social security could enjoy near universal support in Congress.

As the historians filled in this vital part of the story, they realized that even in the fifties the triumph of social security was tempered by the failure to push social insurance into the area of health.

Politics, after all, involved far more than differences across regions; it also concerned state and professional prerogatives. Because of these political forces, social security officials made many compromises even when the program was at the height of its popularity. Disability insurance emerged in 1956 as a program in which administrative responsibilities were divided between the state and the federal government. Health insurance for the aged (Medicare) finally cleared Congress in 1965 in a way that permitted doctors and hospitals total autonomy in their administrative operations and a great deal of control over costs. Congress conceded age groups other than the elderly to private health insurance or welfare.

In these various ways, political scientists, economists, and historians all came to be interested in social security. Thus when Cohen, Myers, and Ball travelled the fiftieth anniversary circuit they were likely to encounter one or more of the academics. The perspectives of the two groups, the participants and the academics, differed in ways that stimulated lively discussions of social security policy.

Influenced by Martha Derthick, the academics often remarked on the control that the participants had over the policy agenda. They argued that Cohen, Ball, Myers, and their colleagues controlled the alternatives and limited choice. To Cohen and Ball, in particular, such suggestions seemed greatly at variance with their experience. First, social security was popular, the people's choice. Second, it had never been as easy for the participants as the academics implied. Even at the height of the Great Society, the participants had needed to convince members of Congress that social security was at least as important a program as the new antipoverty programs. It was, after all, the nation's major antipoverty program. At the same time, they spent, as they had throughout their careers, an inordinate amount of time in difficult discussions of national health insurance in which they far from controlled the policy agenda. Other times brought the challenge of conservative administrations, which often came primed with alternatives to social security. Cohen and Ball achieved continuity in the program but not without effort.

At the same time, some of the academics, particularly the historians, liked to chide the participants for being too conservative. As the title of one book put it, the insiders worked to "insure inequality."[26] Such observations failed to appreciate the difficulties of enacting and preserving large social welfare programs with significant redistributive effects. As just one example, consider the alternative suggestion of 1950 to enact a universal flat pension for the elderly. This suggestion would reemerge in the sixties and seventies in the context of the debate over welfare reform. Just as both liberals and conservatives endorsed universal pensions for the elderly in the fifties, so many embraced a guaranteed annual income for all age groups in the sixties and seventies. The conservatives wanted a modest guarantee on the theory that it would render many other programs unnecessary and hence expendable. The liberals wanted a higher guarantee and tended to see the guaranteed annual income as a supplement to such other programs as social security and medicaid. The guaranteed annual income appealed to some because of its potential to reduce costs and to many others because of its potential to put a safety net under the welfare state. The relevant point is that effective compromise proved impossible between the two groups. It took a great deal for the political system to compromise the differences between liberals and conservatives and to produce new social welfare programs. Those that emerged tended to be narrow in focus and to provide benefits in kind, rather than cash. A program such as food stamps, with its appeal to farmers producing surplus goods, to those who thought that food was a better form of aid than cash, and to those who recognized the program for the cash grant that it really was, was typical. The academics failed to realize that social security, conservative or not, was the only social welfare program that paid high benefits and reached a substantial number of the poor.

Criticism of the social welfare system came easily to the academics: Our welfare system penalizes work and breaks up families; our disability policy encourages retirement rather than rehabilitation; our social security program reduces labor supply and discourages savings; our health insurance system leads to inflation of health care costs; the entire system reflects the world of 1935, with one-wage-earner families, far more than it does the world of 1985.

The dialogue between academics and participants led to the tentative conclusion that, although one could design a better social welfare system, such a system would be impossible to implement.

If social welfare policy were opened up for discussion in today's Congress, for example, the result might be a full-scale retreat from the American version of the welfare state that would leave the system worse than before.

So the participants had learned to be history takers and to accept the less-than-perfect nature of social programs. That made the defense of the social security program all the more important to them. Rather than attempt to pass a new, omnibus social welfare law, a second Social Security Act, they concentrated on incremental improvements in the first Social Security Act. They tended to dwell on subjects such as the benefits received by women in the social security system. Far better, they believed, to talk about such things as sharing wage credits under social security than to explore fundamental alternatives such as the super-IRAs touted by conservatives.

## A PREVIEW

As the fiftieth anniversary came to an end, no one seriously disputed the fact that the old-age insurance program was due to enter a calm period before it faced the difficulties of the baby boom generation's retirement. Most people realized that the social security program would remain as America's major welfare program for some time to come.

Now, then, would appear to be a good time to record the thoughts of the social security participants and to sample some of the recent academic literature. Now would seem a good time to get the story of the first fifty years straight, if for no other reason than to begin to appreciate the contributions of Cohen, and Ball, and Myers and the tradition of nonpartisan, competent administration that they established.

The chapters that follow present a fiftieth anniversary sampler, with a strong historical twist. They capture some of the dialogue between academics and participants that was a feature of the celebration. They give a sense of how academic interest in the subject has grown over the last twenty-five years. They present some alternative visions of social security's future, one by an academic outsider and others by participant insiders.

Chapters 2 and 3 concentrate on the program's history and its reception by historians. Mark Leff writes broadly on how social security has been perceived by the historical profession, emphasizing the myths that have surrounded the program and the difficulties the program encountered in its early years. I then present a case study of how past actions have contributed to the modern program, using the 1939 amendments as an example.

Chapter 4 represents a judicious assessment of how economists have viewed social security over the years. Henry Aaron and Lawrence Thompson occupy a middle ground in the social security dialogue. Not only are they respected economists, but they also have served in influential government posts, Aaron as assistant secretary of Health, Education, and Welfare and Thompson as head of SSA's Office of Research and Statistics. Their essay underscores the way in which starting assumptions influence the conclusions that economists reach.

Chapter 5 moves the volume from intellectual history to a consideration of the program's problems and prospects. Martha Derthick, perhaps the most influential person in the making of the academic renaissance in the social security field, turns her attention to the administrative problems that social security has recently experienced. She describes the flawed efforts to implement Supplemental Security Income and to remove disability beneficiaries from the rolls, and she attempts to account for the apparent deterioration in the quality of administration that these efforts seem to indicate. Her essay is of particular interest in that it allows her to contemplate the effects of the more open policymaking environment that she, in some small way, helped to create.

The remaining two chapters are devoted to the alternative visions of the future of social security. W. Andrew Achenbaum draws on his recent work with the Twentieth Century Fund and his previous work on the history of the elderly in America to propose some fundamental revisions in social security. Appropriately, the volume ends with an essay by Wilbur Cohen and a reply by Robert Myers.

Cohen takes his usual broad and optimistic view of social policy; Myers affectionately takes Cohen to task, not on the broad vision, but on some of the details. Myers agrees with Cohen more than

he disagrees with him. Both recognize that social security represents the most significant achievement in the history of Amercan
social welfare programs.

Even the academics would agree. That is why social security is
worth writing about and even fighting about. That is why part of
the celebration of social security's fiftieth anniversary deserves to
be recorded here and in the chapters that follow. For, as Wilbur
Cohen, Robert Ball, and Robert Myers have always known, social
security is of more than academic interest.

## NOTES

1. Wilbur J. Cohen, *Retirement Policies Under Social Security* (Berke-
ley and Los Angeles: University of California Press, 1958); Robert J.
Myers, *Social Security*, 3d ed. (Homewood, Ill.: Richard D. Irwin, 1985);
Robert Ball, *Social Security: Today and Tomorrow* (New York: Columbia
University Press, 1978).

2. Wilbur Cohen to Joseph P. Harris, American Public Welfare Association, August 19, 1935, RG 47, Records of the Social Security Board,
National Archives, Washington, D.C. (hereafter RG 47); Cohen to Stan-
ley Rector, August 6, 1935, RG 47.

3. *Social Security Bulletin: Annual Statistical Supplement, 1981*, p. 11;
Myers, *Social Security*, p. 224.

4. Robert Pear, "Social Security Marking Golden Anniversary," *New
York Times*, August 14, 1985, p. 1.

5. Quoted in "Social Security Pioneers Recall Program's Birth," *New
York Times*, April 1, 1985, p. A–12.

6. Robert J. Myers, "Social Security: A 50-Year Report Card," prepared by Myers and the Senate Special Committee on Aging and distributed by both.

7. Quoted in Pear, "Social Security Marking Golden Anniversary."

8. Committee on Economic Security, *Social Security in America*
(Washington, D.C.: Government Printing Office, 1937).

9. "Interview with Charles Murray," *New York Times*, April 11, 1986,
p. 18.

10. Senator Proxmire, *Congressional Record*, June 19, 1985, p. S 8347.

11. Pear, "Social Security Marking Golden Anniversary;" *A Fifty Year
Report Card on the Social Security System* (Washington, D.C.: American
Association of Retired Persons, 1985).

12. Lamm quoted in Eric Kingson et al., *The Common Stake: The*

*Interdependence of Generations (A Policy Framework)* (Washington, D.C.: The Gerontological Society, 1986).

13. See Kingson et al., *The Common Stake.*

14. Stockman quoted in W. Andrew Achenbaum, *Social Security: Visions and Revisions* (New York: Cambridge University Press, 1986).

15. "130 Centenarians Get Old Age Aid," *New York Times*, August 14, 1960, p. 58; Tom Wicker, "Social Security Marks 25th Year," *New York Times*, August 14, 1960, p. 59.

16. W. H. Lawrence, "Kennedy Pledges a Drive to Widen Social Security," *New York Times*, August 15, 1960, p. 1.

17. Martha Derthick, *Policymaking for Social Security* (Washington, D.C.: Brookings Institution, 1979); Paul Light, *Artful Work* (New York: Random House, 1985); Gary P. Freeman, "Voters, Bureaucrats, and the State: On the Autonomy of Social Security Policymaking," unpublished paper.

18. Wilbur J. Cohen, "Edwin Witte," in Walter I. Trattner, ed., *Biographical Dictionary of Social Welfare in America* (Westport, Conn.: Greenwood Press, 1986), p. 786.

19. See, for example, Stephen Skowronek, *Building a New American State: The Expansion of National Administrative Capacities, 1877–1920* (New York: Cambridge University Press, 1981); Theda Skocpol and John Ikenberry, "The Political Formation of the American Welfare State in Historical and Comparative Perspective," in Richard P. Tomasson, ed., *Comparative Social Research Annual*, 6 (1983), pp. 87–148.

20. Wicker, "Social Security Marks 25th Year"; Senator Daniel Moynihan, *Congressional Record*, June 19, 1985, p. S 8347.

21. Wilbur Cohen to Arthur Altmeyer, February 10, 1937, RG 47, Box 98, Chairman's Files, File 705, RG 47.

22. Mr. Doughton, *Congressional Record*, October 4, 1949, p. 13820; Mr. Kean, *Congressional Record*, October 4, 1949, p. 13833.

23. Robert S. Lynd and Helen Merrill Lynd, *Middletown: A Study in Modern American Culture* (New York: Harcourt, Brace, and World, 1929), p. 84; *Issues in Social Security*, chap. 1, Report to the House Ways and Means Committee (Washington: Government Printing Office, 1946), reprinted in William Haber and Wilbur J. Cohen, eds., *Readings in Social Security* (New York: Prentice Hall, 1948), p. 247; *Old Age and Survivors Insurance*, Summary, Report to the Senate Committee on Finance from the Advisory Council on Social Security, 80th Congress, 2d Session, 1948, in Haber and Cohen, p. 250; *Recommendations on Coverage and Eligibility for Benefits*, Report to the Senate Committee on Finance from the Advisory Council on Social Security, 1948, in Haber and Cohen, pp. 266–67.

24. Curtis quoted in Arthur Altmeyer, *The Formative Years of Social Security* (Madison: University of Wisconsin Press, 1966), p. 182.

25. See W. Andrew Achenbaum, *Social Security: Visions and Revisions*.

26. Jerry Cates, *Insuring Inequality* (Ann Arbor: University of Michigan Press, 1983).

# 2

# Historical Perspectives on Old-Age Insurance: The State of the Art on the Art of the State

The recent fiftieth anniversary of the Social Security Act marks the first program milestone to which historians have contributed. As recently as ten years ago, the system had received little sustained historical attention from within the academy. The body of literature is still not majestic or definitive, but it is approaching respectability. Historical studies of social security have moved in a number of promising directions, and this anniversary offers a timely opportunity to take stock.

This essay focuses on old-age insurance to the exclusion of the other titles of the Social Security Act (I have even adopted the popular imperialistic practice of using the term social security to refer to what the technicians call OASI—old-age and survivors insurance). This program, after all, is both the pearl and the pillar of the American welfare state, a political marvel that has beaten the ideological odds and has allowed Americans to receive government checks without stigma. As such, its historical development is certainly important enough to merit central attention here. But my choice of subject in truth has a less exalted rationale, reflecting a basic imbalance in the historical literature. It is unfortunate, for example, that no historian has published a full-scale treatment of the unemployment insurance system to carry forward the excellent work of Daniel Nelson.[1]

Even the historical literature on old-age insurance, such as it is, warrants little praise for the historical profession, for we have had so little to do with it. Therefore, it seems only gracious—and honest—to give credit where it is due. Historical sociologists, political scientists, and others have taken the lead in locating the system in broad institutional and political contexts. These social scientists have enabled us to see how such factors as approaches by earlier reformers, power configurations in Congress, and the activities of employees of the Social Security Administration and their allies have molded the development of the program.

Historical understanding of social security also owes a substantial debt to those who have participated directly in social security policy. Few analyses of the early years of the social security system and its international policy context could surpass the breadth and depth of knowledge achieved in the painstaking studies done in the 1930s by Abraham Epstein, Paul Douglas, Isaac Rubinow, and Barbara Armstrong, among others.[2] This tradition of historically grounded analysis has been continued in the pages of the *Social Security Bulletin* and in books by such social security specialists as Eveline Burns, William Haber, Wilbur Cohen, Douglas Brown, Robert Ball, and Robert Myers.[3] Such works succeed in offering far more to historians than an understandably self-congratulatory picture of triumph over adversity. Edwin Witte's account of the development and passage of the Social Security Act draws on his inside position as executive director of the committee that formulated the program to provide what is still (in conjunction with Secretary of Labor Perkins's memoir) the primary treatment of that much-discussed subject.[4] Social Security Board (and later Social Security Administration) Administrator Arthur Altmeyer's memoir has served even his critics as the main guide to the agency, its philosophy, and the limitations of the programs it administered.[5] Most extraordinary as a source of inside information are the Columbia University Oral History Project interviews with more than seventy social security and medicare principals from Congress, the executive branch, concerned interest groups, and, above all, the Social Security Administration itself. Through these insider accounts, the founding generation of social security, which did so much to shape public understanding over the program's first half-century, is now shaping the process of historical assessment itself.

(Indeed, on many occasions, these figures have monitored and assisted historians struggling to make sense of the past. Wilbur Cohen and Robert Myers in particular have done a heroic job of trying to keep us honest.) By drawing upon the insights and experiences of these exceptional individuals, historians have an unusual opportunity to provide a multilayered view of the system's development.

Nor do these inside sources exhaust the interdisciplinary work that can be of assistance to the social security historian. One might consider, for example, the body of literature on the comparative development of the welfare state. By contrasting social insurance systems across countries and over time, this impressive and increasingly systematic literature has cast doubt on many of the more facile explanations for the timing and growth of social security in America. Although some relationships have emerged, such as the positive correlation between the age of a social insurance system and its current share of national income, other explanations have not withstood critical scrutiny. The postulated correlations between economic development and the introduction of the welfare state, or between efforts to respond to working-class challenges and increased social welfare expenditures, have not materialized. Faced with a complex array of variables that includes bureaucratic capacity, paternalistic traditions, political party balance, and the pattern of transferring institutional knowledge and capability from one country to the next, one analyst has concluded, "Public policies are complex phenomena, and humility is desirable in those who seek to discover enduring relationships."[6] In some ways this conclusion makes the work of the historian all the more important. Current work suggests that "universal rules" may best be used to raise possibilities; an understanding of the origins and development of any social insurance system requires sensitivity to historical context, to the governmental structures and previous policy patterns within which political leaders and policy experts must work.[7]

Inundated as we are with insightful analyses, insider accounts, and increasingly sophisticated methodologies, why have historians not contributed more to understanding American social security? In the first place, social welfare history has never occupied a prominent place in the study of American history. Until the "rediscovery" of poverty in the 1960s, the field remained terribly underdeveloped. Furthermore, historians do not rush to judgment, and they often leave contemporary history to others. One should remember that social security has achieved its economic, political, and social prominence only in recent years. As late as the mid–1950s, when old-age insurance expenditures amounted to only 1 percent of the gross national product, the subject did not generate today's burning interest in the growth of the program. Furthermore, the subject of social security is not an easy one for the historian to penetrate; its technical detail and complexity can be intimidating. Finally, there is the fact that, although historians relish the sound, fury, and hand-to-hand combat of political history, they have less appetite for the details of implementation and expansion. It calls to mind an aphorism attributed to Bismarck, "If you like laws and sausages, you should never watch either one being made." In the historian's case, this aphorism should read, "If you like laws and sausages, you should never watch either one after passage."

Still, social security has received attention from historians who study presidents and their reform programs. No history of Franklin Roosevelt's New Deal, to take the most obvious and prominent example, would be complete without a consideration of the social security legislation which FDR considered the "cornerstone of his administration" and of his reform legacy.[8] Social security provides a remarkably revealing glimpse not only of the condition of the elderly in the 1930s but of Roosevelt's debt to previous progressive approaches, his commitment to a more humane state that went beyond palliation, his distaste for the dole, his often-overlooked fiscal conservatism that inclined him toward a self-supporting financing system, and his facility at coopting more radical political forces. The story of social security, in other words, offers a valuable opportunity to provide a fuller, more coherent view of FDR. This view would integrate the welfare-state Roosevelt from whom Ronald Reagan seeks to deliver us and the opponent of government spending and demoralizing "direct relief" whom Reagan loves to quote. How much more satisfying this story would be than the customary treatment of social security history, which slides over such subtleties to focus on Roosevelt as a seer. To do so, capsule histories universally quote the same passage in which FDR defends regressive payroll tax financing as designed to create a sense of earned entitlement so that "no damn politician can ever scrap my social security program." They often neglect to point out that this quotation was the ultimate in Wednesday morning quarterbacking, delivered six years after the act's passage (many of us would appear more farsighted if given six years to winnow our earlier predictions and select the rationale that had proven most accurate and least ephemeral). One can understand the modern temptation to simplify the program's history by claiming that its strengths had been carefully engineered from the outset, but this should not be allowed to obscure the more textured picture of the program's origins that New Deal historians have provided.[9]

Therefore, I do not find myself in particular sympathy with those who suggest that public policy historians should make a complete shift from presidential administrations to analyses of particular problems. Eash has its place. The broad domestic constraints on the Truman administration, for example, have been ably demonstrated in a study of the administration's efforts to pass national health insurance.[10] Although little has been done on the way that the Eisenhower administration handled the social security issue, such study would clarify not only the program's development but also the broader administration role in the expansion of the welfare state. The special position of old-age insurance in the American social welfare effort, for example, becomes clearer when reading the minutes of the Eisenhower cabinet, where social security was extolled as a "humane, forward, yet not New Dealish" program, founded on conservative principles of self-reliance, that could hinder the growth of noncontributory pensions.[11] Ike highlighted this new Republican theme himself in campaign speeches that repeatedly boasted of his administration's expansion of social security.[12]

No one who encounters Eisenhower's collected wisdom on social security would accuse him of great interest in it or even of any depth of understanding about how it worked. On the other hand, further study seems certain to validate Ike's emerging reputation for political acumen.[13] The cabinet discussions that clinched administrative support for a greatly expanded program characterized the so-called Chamber of Commerce proposal for a noncontributory flat pension as "bad math" and a "numbers racket . . . we would always lose." This alternative to social security, supported by many Republicans such as Nebraska's Carl Curtis, offered more adequate provision for several million Americans, but it threatened to alienate a far larger group who had developed a commitment to the existing program.[14] Ike later put it more directly, dismissing a suggested flat rejection of a Democratic proposal to raise benefits with the declaration, if we "just say no, we'll get rolled."[15]

Even from the perspective of the much-maligned "presidential synthesis," the need for a more systematic and wide-ranging study of the social security system becomes apparent. As much as we need to understand the political context in order to understand the program, the reverse is also true. The social security literature demonstrates that the currents that have pushed the social security system forward do not follow independent presidential direction. Instead, presidential decisions themselves are constrained by the program's momentum and by agendas set and alternatives debated at lower levels. It becomes necessary, then, to examine social security not only at peak moments of political conflict, change, and crisis, but also at more mundane times.

This approach has underpinned the most recent historical studies of social security, just in the nick of time. As old-age insurance and its financial "crisis" moved to the center of political attention, history had a classic role to play: helping to answer the questions of the present by reference to the record of the past. Until quite recently, historians had regrettably little to offer. Although social welfare history had become a growth industry by the 1970s, its practitioners generally searched in the distant, pre–social security past for American social welfare attitudes and approaches. Social security was not so much left behind as placed ahead of the discussion. Otherwise, American historians could only direct questioners to the insider memoirs of Witte, Altmeyer, and Perkins, to an excellent biography of Witte which owed its origins to the author's interest in the Wisconsin school of social reform, and to the sketchy historical overviews done in other fields.[16] In the history of presidential administrations, old-age insurance had usually received only scattered sentences, most of them on the passage of the 1935 act. The twists and turns of the program, to say nothing of its place in the broader sweep of American political history, remained largely unexplored; even in the historian's familiar realm of legislative history, the crucial 1939 and 1950 amendments seldom made it into print. Until quite recently, these gaps loomed large.

Circumstances have changed, and historical questions are eliciting extended and systematic historical answers, even if not from the historical profession. Over the last seven years, three books, as well as a number of more delimited studies, have appeared on the history of old-age insurance. Two questions have received particular attention. The first focuses on the unusual American decision to finance social security exclusively with regressive payroll taxes. This decision invites consideration of what some perceive to be the program's inadequate contribution to income redistribution. Arguing that "the policies in place fail to protect those most in need while they provide extensive protection where it is least needed,"[17] such studies note the role of social security in "insuring inequality." The authors of these studies seek to determine the origins and development of this perceived failure of income redistribution (a concern that unites neoliberals who wish to target federal funds more efficiently and conservatives who wish to reserve government aid for the most needy and to limit the government's social welfare responsibilities and reduce its expenditures).[18] In part because of the political ambiguity of such critiques, the premise that social security could have been more redistributive often angers the program's current defenders, but even they are coming to recognize that investigating this redistributive issue can enrich our understanding of social security.

The redistribution question takes second place these days to the loaded question of how the program got to be so large and uncontrollable. Political scientist Martha Derthick and economist Carolyn Weaver have addressed this question in recent books.[19] Derthick's brilliant, masterful study justifiably dominates the field of social security history. It covers so much ground so well and with such evident sophistication that it tends to intimidate potential entrants into the field, who have every reason to be awed by Derthick's command of the subject. Encompassing the political role of the Social Security Administration, congressional committees, the executive branch, interest groups, social security experts, and the broader public, Derthick subtly describes the techniques and interrelationships contributing to the politics of incremental expansion that she sees at the heart of the social security policy-making system.

Carolyn Weaver's provocative study, designed to use social security "to provide insight into the general process of government growth," has more obvious weaknesses.[20] Historians tend to have difficulties when an ahistorical model, in this case the public choice model, is applied to the past and declared to be a perfect fit. The development of social security resists such "universal" rules. One suspects, for example, that consultation of the Columbia oral history interviews and archival research might have tempered some of her conclusions. As matters stand, crucial causal factors in Weaver's analysis remain more in the realm of assumption than of evidence. These factors include the drive for power and jobs that supposedly propelled the "reformer zealots," the complex calculations of prospective rates of return that allegedly guided public opinion on the program, the claim that "political accept-ance" hinged on the misleading private insurance analogy, and the belief that the reformer monopoly of resources and incentives blocked conservatives from effectively presenting the persuasive case for free-market solutions.[21] Weaver tends to shortchange evi-dence that runs contrary to her model, such as the failure to expand social security in the 1940s and the constant pressure for Townsend-like alternatives to social security, which persisted into the 1950s. Yet her contributions outweigh such shortcomings. Not only has she brought together legislative and other material on old-age in-surance to provide a coherent, chronologically organized narrative of social security over its entire history, she has also sensitized us to a wide range of public policy explanations that will continue to influence and inform research.

This necessarily brief and sketchy review of the literature on the history of the old-age insurance program helps to launch an ex-amination of the most promising paths to further work in social security.[22] The first rule of the road is that anything approximating a monocausal explanation is a dead end. In this regard, Frances Piven and Richard Cloward's *Regulating the Poor* comes to mind. In this exciting and influential book, they argue that the welfare state performs the functions of restoration of "social control," "political 'reintegration' of disaffected groups," and protection of "the work system." The system expands to quell social disorder and change and contracts "when peace and order reign."[23] Piven and Cloward's combative challenge to conventional wisdom works better as a general insight than as a guide to particular situations and programs. In the case of social security, the thesis helps to explain the Social Security Act as a response to the Townsend movement and other powerful social crusades. On the other hand, no one can deny that a great deal more was involved in the creation of social security; beyond the events of 1935, the applicability of the Piven and Cloward thesis only deteriorates. To cite only the most obvious example, the program expanded after the return of peace and order. In fact, one is tempted to reverse the terms of the analysis and argue that the more peace and order, the greater the expansion of the program, yet that too would be too simple. In response to criticisms of their work by historians, Piven and Cloward issued a disclaimer. Their book was about "people in the labor force, not about those exempted from the necessity of working." So much for the social control thesis as a key to social security history.[24]

A more sophisticated application of labor market theory has since gained sway, but this one also proves unsatisfying and offers an incomplete picture of the program. William Graebner, in a highly impressive history of retirement, has argued that old-age insurance, like the employee pension systems for colleges, railroads, and federal workers, must be understood as a conscious effort to push older people out of the labor force to make way for younger, more efficient workers. Even beyond the grace with which Graebner presents it, this thesis has inherent appeal; social security has indeed accelerated retirements, and intention is always the most satisfying way of accounting for results. Graebner does show that certain key researchers who contributed to old-age insurance, such as Barbara Armstrong, shared an industrial relations approach that emphasized the desirability of retiring "superannuated" surplus workers, and he makes a good case that the "retirement test" in particular owed much to their efforts. But he is too good a historian to fail to note that his corroborating evidence is at times "conflicting" and in general "not all that plentiful." One has to search long and hard in both the administrative and congressional consideration of social security for the very scattered references to this retirement argument. Even then, the objective sometimes proves not to be to retire the elderly but to assure that their pensions would not allow them to underbid younger workers for jobs. Despite the logical appeal of freeing up work spaces for the unemployed in time of depression, one should not forget what Graebner himself realizes: that old age pensions were not scheduled to be paid until six and a half years after the enactment of the legislation, and the scheduled initial low pensions could scarcely have been expected to create a mass exodus from the work force.[25] At best, it seems, this labor market argument played a peripheral role in the passage of old-age insurance or in its content, with the notable exception of the retirement test. For an adequate understanding of social security, we have to look elsewhere.

Labor market theories imply regulation that serves the interest of the ruling class, and the conception of social security as an instrument of class power does have its defenders. This argument, although it takes a different form than those of Piven and Cloward and Graebner, emerges as no more convincing. Advocates of the "corporate liberal" explanation of American reform believe that farseeing members of the business elite use social legislation to head off radical popular challenges and to stabilize production and employment to their own benefit. The passage of social security often figures prominently as a case study that proponents claim validates the theory.[26] These proponents recite a highly publicized endorsement of social security by the Commerce Department's Business Advisory Council. In so doing, they dismiss or neglect the facts that the endorsement referred to the "general principles" of old-age insurance, rather than its actual provisions, that many members of the council had serious objections, that the council did not represent the business community as a whole or even this country's business elite, that the council soon dissolved in an acid bath of resignations in partial protest of the president's perceived exploitation of this lukewarm endorsement, and that presentation of a half-hearted report scarcely constitutes business responsibility for the legislation.

Even more recent, well-researched, sophisticated versions of this corporate liberal argument fall short. The evidence has its persuasive aspects: Some welfare capitalists had implemented industrial pension plans for their employees; some of these corporate leaders, who were consulted in drawing up the old-age insurance program, felt that similar plans should be adopted on a national scale. Social security did have characteristics in common with the earlier corporate plans, such as wage-related benefits and the very fact of introducing public pensions through private labor markets. Even here, however, it is important not to confuse correlation and causality. Private pensions were a model for social security, but that does not imply that private business leaders were responsible for the passage of the Social Security Act in 1935 or for its contents.[27] Welfare capitalists all too clearly had only a marginal role to play in the program's formulation and adoption. The very fact that their views, and not the views of other business leaders, received a hearing indicated that more basic forces were at work.[28] This more complex picture demands historical attention.

Raising monocausal interpretations and dismissing them as reductionist, the historical profession appears at times to be chasing its own tail. It comes up with theories that defy common sense and then triumphantly dismantles them. In part, this futile tendency stems from the weakness of what might be called the conventional wisdom. Alternatives, even weak ones, become more attractive than the story as it is generally told.

Old-age insurance is often depicted as a simple response to public demands, born of the depression-era recognition of old-age dependency and shaped by the American belief in self-reliance, the work ethic, the free market, and "getting what you pay for." In order to carve social security out of a "liberal mold," the program allowed each worker to use his own thrift and establish, in J. Douglas Brown's words, "an earned contractual right to his own annuity."[29] This action freed the program "from overtones of state paternalism as well as from any socialist ideologies of redistribution."[30] Numerous quotations from Franklin Roosevelt and his successors reinforce this point, and few doubt that the insurance imagery of social security has helped to build a fierce sense of entitlement that protects the program from what Martha Derthick might call the routines of politics. The insurance model, in other words, matched American values and sustained the program.

A closer reading of the early history of old-age insurance leaves open the possibility that these broader public values did not determine the initial content of social security however much they may have contributed to the later growth of old-age insurance.[31] Historians agree, for example, that payroll tax-financed old-age insurance was not the public's choice in 1935. The vigorous public and congressional demand for federal action to deal with the plight of the elderly focused on more immediate and direct means of relief, such as what ultimately became Title I of the Social Security Act. Old-age assistance, which provided federal matching grants for state, means-tested, noncontributory payments to the elderly, was not securely grounded in any of the "traditional American values" that are said to explain the American attachment to social security. One did not get what one paid for, and it was not an exercise in insurance or self-reliance. If anything, it encouraged "indolence" by linking payment to low incomes. At best, it could be said to resemble existing federal social welfare programs, such as veterans pensions, and thus to partake of the welfare, not the working, traditions of this country. For all of that, informed sources agree that Title I was the most popular title in the Social Security Act.

Many people believed at the time, and today's historians tend to agree, that old-age insurance would not have passed without old-age assistance. If FDR had not insisted on "bundling" old-age insurance and old-age assistance in an all or nothing offer, today's social security program might have died on the vine.[32] Nor should this preference for a means-tested program over social insurance surprise us. Contributory social insurance could not by definition have provided for the aged victims of the depression who had not earned an annuity. In this time as well the traditional indictment of government handouts as a demoralizing narcotic that sapped independence lost its bite, particularly as applied to the far-from-shiftless retired elderly. Squeezed out of the labor force, the elderly needed little defense as to their commitment to the work ethic. Abstract free-market principles gave way to tangible efforts to make more adequate provision for the basic needs of the elderly.

Once social security is seen as aid to the elderly rather than as a remote expression of free-market principles, the early history of the program falls into place. The "insurance model" of social security—exclusive reliance on payroll taxes analogous to insurance "premiums," each worker's "annuity" scaled to past contributions, payments to each generation based on the taxes already collected from them—was a "casualty" of this mindset, and in a perverse sense of the word; Congress and the broader public were quite "casual" in casting it aside. This phenomenon has to do with more than the political influence of mass movements on behalf of non-contributory old-age pensions. Public opinion polls for the early years of social security register one-sided support for the program and for its payroll taxes, yet they provide no evidence that this endorsement derived from the themes of self-reliance and "earned right" insurance. A rise in benefit levels, vastly in excess of any individual's accrued contributions, had great appeal. A large share of the public that so loyally embraced social security did not even know that their own payroll-tax payments would automatically entitle them to a retirement pension.[33] Even as this connection sunk in, the sense of entitlement among the elderly extended beyond a reclaiming of past tax benefits: they had earned the right to a decent pension through their contributions to society, of which their social security contributions reflected only a part.

No wonder, then, that Congress in 1939 so cavalierly undermined the system's previous precarious financial balance: boosting benefits for early annuitants even further beyond what their accumulated tax payments would have justified, extending benefits to survivors, loosening the already less-than-rigorous relationship between what an individual paid and what he or she was likely to receive, and postponing the scheduled tax increase without even taking the trouble to map out an alternative means of balancing the program's books in the future.[34] Even this action soon proved insufficient. Both the 1940 Democratic platform and Roosevelt himself talked about establishing a universal minimum benefit, and in response to such pressures, so-called double-decker plans were drafted. On the first deck would be a basic pension, and on top of that would come benefits earned through social insurance. In fact, until Eisenhower killed the idea of a universal flat pension in 1954, this alternative to social insurance was considered a primary threat to the social security program. As one presidential staff memorandum put it in 1949, "The race between insurance and pensions" was still "nip and tuck."[35] This concern anchors the recollections of Arthur Altmeyer, who is echoed by many of his subordinates. Altmeyer explains that congressional challenges to contributory, wage-related principles were so great that "We were fortunate that the committees with which we had to deal were money-minded committees. Otherwise we would have had a flat general pension. There's no question about that."[36]

Although Congress protected the principles of social insurance, it failed to uphold the financing scheme on which self-financed social insurance rested. Not only in 1939, but seven more times between 1942 and 1947, Congress turned back scheduled payroll taxes increases, over the vocal opposition of the Social Security Board/Administration (SSB/SSA). If the social insurance model had been sacrosanct, such congressional challenges to the preferences of the program administrators would not have prevailed. Similar logic could be applied to the willingness of Congress in the late 1930s and 1940s to allow for the future use of general revenue subsidies, even though that would further attenuate the resemblance between social security and private insurance. In the forties, Congress and the social security administrators regarded an eventual government subsidy to the program's coffers as inevitable, and Congress even passed a law in 1944 that allowed for such a subsidy should it become necessary to cover future benefit payments.

If these actions do not suggest a sense of social responsibility to the elderly that went beyond an insurance mentality, then one is well-advised to examine the early years of the old-age assistance program. This state-run, federally assisted welfare program has received little attention from historians, with the exception of Jerry Cates who has chronicled the Social Security Board's response to the challenge that old-age assistance posed to social security.[37] In many ways, the welfare program proved far more vigorous than did the social insurance program during the years between 1935 and 1950. Many found old-age assistance to be too vigorous, complaining of the "political attraction" and "irresponsible expansion" in some states of this "give-away" program. By the end of the forties, for example, just over a fifth of the elderly received OAA payments, and in a few states it was over half. Low as old age assistance benefit levels were and as inconsistent as they were from state to state, they more than doubled between 1939 and 1950, averaging 70 percent higher than old-age insurance payments.

American old-age insurance thus spent its youth not in the cozy womb of supportive conservative free-market values but in an environment that challenged its inadequacies. Sometimes these pressures, ironically, pushed the program toward a self-protective conservatism; the sanctification of fiscal soundness and insurance principles was partly designed to block proposals for excessive pensions from being grafted onto the program.[38] More obviously, this challenge brought liberalization in the crucial early amendments to social security. To raise benefit levels and start money flowing sooner, the 1939 amendments moved away from self-contained and long-term financing;[39] to raise benefit levels beyond those of public assistance and to overcome the advantage that public assistance enjoyed in terms of coverage, the 1950 amendments elevated benefit levels and greatly expanded social insurance coverage.

None of these arguments disputes the recognition that the insurance analogy contributed to the political support for social security expansion or its insulation from political routine. Instead, they underscore the distortions and omissions that can result from assuming the program's past on the basis of the present. In this case, as in so many others, history turns out not to be that simple. Much of the conventional wisdom on social security applies to events after 1954 far more neatly than before that date.

Here the nonhistorian may be tempted to ask: So what? If the formula for expansion and support of the insurance principle can better be traced to the early 1950s than to the 1930s, who really cares? Historians, by the nature of their discipline, do not have the luxury of simply dismissing the past, and there are a number of reasons for bringing the past back into policy discussions of social security.

In the first place, historians realize that the insurance principle claimed numerous victims during its "maturation" period. As late as the early 1950s, two-thirds of the elderly still received no old-age insurance benefits, and over one-and-a-half million of those were found to be receiving no public assistance despite having no money income of their own.[40] Millions in addition had received inadequate assistance far below the popular minimum flat pensions then being put forward. The insurance logic of the social security system, and the premium on fiscal discipline that accompanied it, had taken a terrible toll—one that can be confirmed in the most tragic fashion both by income distribution statistics that located a heavily disproportionate share of the aged at the very bottom, and by the countless pleas to congressmen sent by elderly Americans in this period.[41]

In the second place, one could extend this temporal argument, and put it on a more permanent basis, by arguing that the politically viable roads taken had enduring consequences for the broader growth of the American welfare state. Assistance to the retired elderly, the welfare program with the greatest popular support, could presumably have legitimated a broad range of welfare state programs. Even in the case of the old-age insurance approach that did triumph, parallels to noncontributory programs could have been made. Recipients' insurance "annuities" vastly exceeded the actuarial value of past contributions, in effect awarding those recipients subsidies from current payroll tax collections that were often well in excess of the subsidies from general revenues received by welfare clients. Despite these subsidies, old-age insurance was justified, and eventually accepted, in terms of a distinction between earned insurance and unearned welfare. That rationale, Theda Skocpol and Jerry Cates suggest, may have been neither politically necessary nor healthy for the growth of other social welfare programs.[42] "Getting what you pay for" does not seem relevant, for example, to the problems of helping a child out of poverty. The less carefully drawn insurance/welfare distinction in other countries has arguably eased those countries' acceptance of such programs as family allowances and health insurance, even though one must keep in mind the international experience that suggests the inherent long-term political vulnerability of means-tested programs.

Whether one accepts these arguments, one can at least recognize the inadequacy of a popular pressures explanation of social security and accept the fact that history has consequences. Granting that, one is still left with major questions about who played the crucial role in the development of old-age insurance. Here recent scholarship provides an answer: The major candidate for the role of crucial actor in the development of old-age insurance is the Social Security Administration itself. It always turns up where the action is. This conclusion should not be surprising. Historical study of social welfare programs in Europe suggests a similar preeminent bureaucratic role in identifying areas of possible expansion and pushing them forward.[43]

In the pluralistic United States, however, such bureaucratic success seems more remarkable, almost a conspiracy against the American style of government. Indeed, Jerry Cates and Carolyn Weaver have played on conspiratorial themes in their recent monographs. Relying predominantly on an intensive analysis of the papers of the Social Security Administration between 1935 and 1954, Jerry Cates presents an unflattering view of SSB/SSA leaders conspiring to limit the program's redistributive potential. He shows SSB/SSA officialdom undertaking a public relations campaign that idealized insurance imagery at the expense of the public assistance program, maintaining internal orthodoxy by suppressing points of view critical of old-age insurance's regressive features, and waging a systematic effort to limit liberalization of means-testing for state old-age assistance to prevent it from being a stronger competitor to old-age insurance. More measured analyses indicate that he has overstated his case. SSB/SSA leaders undoubtedly were obsessed, for both ideological and strategic reasons, with protecting old-age insurance against overly generous minimum pension schemes that might ultimately crowd out contributory wage-related features. Yet these efforts did not always reflect "redistribution-limiting" motivations and an "anti-poor bias." Such motivations do not easily square, for example, with the SSB/SSA's advocacy in the late 1930s and 1940s of future government supplements to old-age insurance payroll taxes, with their often justified fear that flat plans were designed to reduce the overall future federal commitment to the aged, and more broadly, with their belief that a successful old-age insurance program would ultimately serve the best interests not only of the nation as a whole but of the poor in particular.

Whatever questions one can direct at Cates's conclusions, his evidence unmistakably shows the SSB/SSA playing a central role in framing the social security issue and in damage-limitation efforts to deal with threatening alternatives from outside of the bureaucratic circles. Carolyn Weaver joins Cates in casting SSB/SSA leaders in a villainous central role, but one that is almost a mirror-image of Cates's characterization. Her bureaucrat/zealots pursue evil redistribution while promoting their own self-interest and the program's overexpansion. They pack expert committees, shamelessly exploit "misleading insurance terminology," and selectively bias "information made available . . . to citizens and legislators," thus using their "monopoly power" to seize control of the political agenda.[44]

Both Cates and Weaver follow the lead of Martha Derthick in placing the SSB/SSA at the vortex of social security politics. Derthick more convincingly and comprehensively describes the process by which the SSB/SSA exerted influence and gained its reputation as one of Washington's most skilled, politically sophisticated, and effective bureaucracies. Her book covers the gamut of techniques of influence, showing how the SSA "energized" other actors to forward its own ends: molding advisory councils, collaborating with the American Federation of Labor, parlaying technical expertise into domination of political executives or effective independence from them, and developing close relationships with key congressional committee decision makers. In the process, Derthick demonstrates the effectiveness of the SSA's "subtle blend of adaptation and manipulation," its recognition of when concessions are necessary, and its farsighted sensitivity to the program's future salability. The characteristics of the program itself, particularly a technicality that verged on incomprehensibility, allowed scope for the SSA leaders' exceptional skills in persuasion. Derthick shows them exploiting ambiguities in the program to obscure the way it actually worked (such as the weak relationship between benefits and accumulated taxes) and juggling various program components to enhance overall appeal (such as controlling the spread between maximum and minimum benefits). She is particularly good at describing the SSA's extraordinarily successful use, in the program's glory years between 1950 and the early 1970s, of the strategy of incremental expansion.[45] A stark picture emerges. Social security substantiates, some feel conclusively, the ascendant interpretation of the history of twentieth-century public policy. In this interpretation, policy is not the vector sum of public demands and it is not some magically achieved function of the needs of the economic and social system to stabilize itself; instead, it is more indicative of the way that states shape society rather than vice versa.

Even in arguing for the centrality of the SSB/SSA in social security policymaking, Derthick throughout her book underscores the benefits of a multifaceted approach. The very technique of adaptation, which she describes so well, implies exogenous forces at work. Examples abound. One cannot understand the 1939 amendments without an understanding of popular and interest group pressures. The early financial framework of the social security trust fund can be comprehended only in terms of President Roosevelt's and Henry Morgenthau's fiscally conservative priorities.[46] The congressional resuscitation of old-age insurance and its tax schemes in the 1950 amendments indicates, among other things, the critical role of the Ways and Means Committee and its leaders. Indeed, the financial framework of the evolving program can be traced to priorities of the Ways and Means Committee and particularly to Chairman Wilbur Mills.

This list could go on indefinitely, clinching the point. Public policy analysis is an intricate process encompassing a range of actors and influences, and recent historical study of social security has helped to identify those factors, to weigh their relative importance, and to begin to examine their interrelationships. Historical scholarship has called the quest for universal explanations into question, drawn attention to the heavy hand of the past, and made people aware of the changing historical context of social security.[47]

As this body of work expands, we are becoming aware of the continuities and discontinuities that have defined the social security program. We realize, for example, the importance of digging deeper than the depression to understand the original form of social security. The assumptions of the system's founders that generated the menu of options from which they crafted social security were informed by the ideas of the "Wisconsin school" of institutional economists and by other influences as well.[48] We also are coming to an understanding of the discontinuities in social security history. Only recently, for example, have we appreciated the unique characteristics of the period of relatively conflict-free program expansion from 1950 to the early 1970s. The convergence of a growing economy and a still-maturing program allowed for an almost painless procession of rising benefits that only later would take on a "sorcerer's apprentice" image of uncontrollability. Historians have learned that this experience, as well as the erosion of debate over core program assumptions that accompanied it, has obscured the dissension over certain of these fundamental assumptions in the 1930s and 1940s. That early period, in which the nascent program had not yet built up a "critical mass" of beneficiaries and loyalists, had a very different dynamic. And no one following the social security debate of the last decade can fail to recognize that the easy choices and the studied ambiguity as to how the program actually operated are a problematic legacy. The preceding "golden age" has proved to be unsustainable, as the declining ratio of contributing workers to retiree beneficiaries has given the program less maneuvering room to cope with economic downturns, and has placed program operations more than ever in the goldfish bowl of American politics. In fact, historians have increasingly joined other analysts in focusing on the value decisions that the system has never fully confronted, such as the divisions of responsibility between generations or between the public and private sectors.[49]

The modern social security system emerges from such studies as less than the simple product of a half century of accumulated wisdom and careful calculation; it instead bears the marks of decisions *not* made and developments not universally understood. It is certainly incumbent on a historian of social security to identify the set of expectations, perceptions, and policy patterns that have nourished the program, and that future policymakers can ignore only at their peril. But recent work indicates that historians can move beyond warnings of historical constraints to point to historical possibilities that have not yet been fully explored.

It seems natural, then, to end on a note of scholarly optimism. When the next major anniversaries arrive, and social security reaches the age when *it* could qualify for old-age insurance, historians may well be able to look back on a period of increased contributions to policy debates and a more comprehensive, fully developed picture of the program's history.

The advance in quantity alone is sure to be substantial. Public policy history shows every indication of emerging as a "hot" field in our discipline. And the history of social security, despite the program's intricacy, is hotter yet, thanks to the program's commanding position in the budget and the welfare state.

Hot fields, of course, have a habit of generating more heat than light, and more words than wisdom. In the course of filling the considerable gaps in our historical knowledge of social security, there is of course some danger of inundation from historical accounts that fail to contribute to resolving broader questions and that add little more than clutter and background noise to the understanding of the program. But even to raise that prospective peril is to recognize why there is some reason for optimism that the quality of our knowledge will advance with the quantity. Future historians are unlikely to ignore such factors as the central but changing role of the Social Security Administration, the dangers of reductionist explanations, the political dynamics generated by the program itself, the long-standing political failure to come to grips with the way that social security actually operates, the complex relationship of social security reform to public values and pressures, and the discontinuous contexts that have determined the program's changing direction. Nor does one have to fall back on the platitude that more research is needed. Certainly it is, but some of that research is already under way, and some is on the verge of being published.

The timing for more vigorous examination is propitious. The heyday of incremental expansion of the social security system has passed, and, as a consequence, the nature of some fundamental program issues has become clearer, as have the relationships between social security and other American social welfare programs. As the passage of time affords historians their much-coveted historical distance, one can confidently expect the profession to excavate and illuminate those issues in the coming years. Social security is a middle-aged program; contributions from historians to the program are just gathering steam.

## NOTES

1. Daniel Nelson, *Unemployment Compensation: The American Experience, 1915–1935* (Madison: University of Wisconsin Press, 1969).

2. Abraham Epstein, *Insecurity: A Challenge to America* (New York: Smith and Hass, 1933); Paul H. Douglas, *Social Security in America* (New York: McGraw Hill, 1936); I. M. Rubinow, *The Quest for Security* (New York: Henry Holt, 1934); Barbara M. Armstrong, *Insuring the Essentials* (New York: Macmillan, 1932).

3. Robert J. Myers, *Social Security* (Homewood, Ill.: Richard D. Irwin, 1985); J. Douglas Brown, *The Genesis of the American Social Security System* (Princeton: Industrial Relations Section, 1977); Wilbur J. Cohen, *Retirement Under Social Security* (Berkeley: University of California Press, 1968); Robert M. Ball, *Social Security: Today and Tomorrow* (New

York: Columbia University Press, 1978); William Haber and Wilbur Cohen, eds., *Social Security: Programs, Problems and Policies* (Homewood, Ill.: Richard D. Irwin, 1960); Eveline Burns, *The American Social Security System* (Boston: Houghton Mifflin, 1949).

4. Edwin E. Witte, *The Development of the Social Security Act* (Madison: University of Wisconsin Press, 1963).

5. Athur J. Altmeyer, *The Formative Years of Social Security* (Madison: University of Wisconsin Press, 1966).

6. Arnold J. Heidenheimer et al., *Comparative Public Policy*, 2d ed. (New York: St. Martin's Press, 1983), p. 213.

7. Ann Shola Orloff and Theda Skocpol, "Why Not Equal Protection?" *American Sociological Review* 49 (December 1984), pp. 726–50.

8. Frances Perkins, *The Roosevelt I Knew* (New York: Viking Press, 1946), pp. 188–89, 282–85.

9. Arthur M. Schlesinger, Jr., *The Coming of the New Deal* (Boston: Houghton Mifflin, 1959), pp. 308–15; and Irving Bernstein, *A Caring Society* (Boston: Houghton Mifflin, 1985), which offers a particularly extensive treatment.

10. Monte M. Poen, *Harry S. Truman versus the Medical Lobby* (Columbia: University of Missouri Press, 1979).

11. Folder "C–8 (4), November 20, 1953," White House Office, Office of the Staff Secretary, Cabinet Series, Box 1, Dwight D. Eisenhower Library, Abilene, Kansas.

12. Gary W. Reichard, *The Reaffirmation of Republicanism* (Knoxville: University of Tennessee Press, 1975).

13. Fred Greenstein, *The Hidden Hand Presidency: Eisenhower as Leader* (New York: Basic Books, 1982).

14. Folders "C–9 (3), December 15, 1953," pp. 78–79 and "C–8 (4), November 20, 1953," p. 56, both in Box 1, White House Office, Office of the Staff Secretary, Cabinet Series, Eisenhower Library.

15. Folder "L–49 (3), June 10, 1958," p. 45, White House Office, Legislative Meetings Series, Box 5, Eisenhower Library.

16. Theron F. Schlabach, *Edwin E. Witte: Cautious Reformer* (Madison: Wisconsin State Historical Society, 1969).

17. Gaston V. Rimlinger, "Social Security in Trouble: A World View," p. 1, to be published in Richard Tomasson et al., eds., *Social Security: The First Half Century* (Albuquerque: University of New Mexico Press, 1986).

18. Jerry Cates, *Insuring Inequality: Administrative Leadership in Social Security, 1935–54* (Ann Arbor: University of Michigan Press, 1983); Martha Ozawa, "Income Redistribution and Social Security," *Social Service Review* 50 (June 1976), pp. 210–35.

19. Martha Derthick, *Policymaking for Social Security* (Washington, D.C.: Brookings Institution, 1979); Carolyn L. Weaver, *The Crisis in Social Security* (Durham, N.C.: Duke University Press, 1982). It is worth mentioning that Weaver, a public choice economist, started her book as a doctoral dissertation and accepted a post with Senator Robert Dole and the Senate Finance Committee as the book was going to press. Her book therefore preceded her status as a policy insider.

20. Weaver, p. 195.

21. Ibid., pp. 10 and 15; Carolyn L. Weaver, "The Economics and Politics of the Emergence of Social Security: Some Implications for Reform," *Cato Journal* 3 (Fall 1983), pp. 375, 369–70. Professor Weaver did consult the material in the archives of the HHS Departmental Library (which was the HEW library when she did her research). This library contains files of unpublished speeches by Arthur Altmeyer, Wilbur Cohen, and others. The contrast with Derthick, however, remains striking. Derthick cites the Columbia interviews extensively, and she spent a great deal of time in the Washington National Records Center.

22. To fill the gaps, I recommend Walter I. Trattner and W. Andrew Achenbaum, eds., *Social Welfare in America: An Annotated Bibliography* (Westport, Conn.: Greenwood Press, 1983).

23. Frances Fox Piven and Richard Cloward, *Regulating the Poor* (New York: Random House, 1971), pp. 7, 40, 177, 347.

24. See the essays in Walter Trattner, ed., *Social Welfare or Social Control* (Knoxville: University of Tennessee Press, 1983), particularly the essay by W. Andrew Achenbaum and the response by Piven and Cloward (pp. 67–89, 138). See also the elaborations on the initial theory, such as Piven and Cloward, *Poor People's Movements: Why They Succeed and How They Fail* (New York: Random House, 1977), and the critique of the limited applicability of narrow "political conflict" models in Philip K. Armour and Richard M. Coughlin, "Social Control and Social Security," *Social Science Quarterly* 66 (December 1985), p. 775.

25. William Graebner, *A History of Retirement* (New Haven: Yale University Press, 1980) and William Graebner, "From Pensions to Social Security," in John N. Schacht, ed., *The Quest for Security* (Iowa City: Center for the Study of the Recent History of the United States, 1982), p. 28.

26. Among many examples see William Domhoff, *The Higher Circles* (New York: Random House, 1970), pp. 207–18; Edward S. Greenberg, *Serving the Few* (New York: Wiley, 1974), p. 174; Kim McQuaid, *Big Business and Presidential Power* (New York: Morrow, 1982).

27. Jill S. Quadagno, "Welfare Capitalism and the Social Security Act of 1935," *American Sociological Review* 49 (October 1984), pp. 632–37;

Edward Berkowitz and Kim McQuaid, *Creating the Welfare State: The Political Economy of Twentieth Century Reform* (New York: Praeger, 1980). [Editor's note: Berkowitz and McQuaid attempt an organizational survey of social welfare programs that emphasized the relationship between the public and private sectors. Although corporate leaders preceded public bureaucrats into the field of old-age pensions, Berkowitz and McQuaid recognize that, by the end of the thirties, a distinctively public approach to social welfare had developed. In subsequent work, Berkowitz has expanded on the meaning of this "public" approach.]

28. Theda Skocpol and Edwin Amenta, "Did Capitalists Shape Social Security," *American Sociological Review* 50 (August 1985), pp. 572–74.

29. Brown quoted in Gaston V. Rimlinger, *Welfare Policy and Industrialization* (New York: John Wiley & Sons, 1971), pp. 193, 230.

30. Gaston V. Rimlinger, "Social Security in Trouble: A World View," p. 6, to be published in Richard Tomasson et al., eds., *Social Security: The First Half Century* (Albuquerque: University of New Mexico Press, 1986).

31. See the wide-ranging and insightful critique of the "Democratic Politics Model" in Gary P. Freeman, "Voters, Bureaucrats, and the State: On the Autonomy of Social Security Policymaking," to be published in *Social Security: The First Half Century*.

32. Carolyn Weaver, "The Economics and Politics of the Emergence of Social Security: Some Implications for Reform," *Cato Journal* 3 (Fall 1983), p. 376.

33. Michael Schiltz, *Public Attitudes toward Social Security, 1935–1965* (Washington: Government Printing Office, 1970), pp. 83–87.

34. This paragraph and the next one draw on my examination of the payroll tax freeze in "Speculating in Social Security Futures," to be published in *Social Security: The First Half Century*.

35. Staff comments, "Expansion and Extension of the Social Security System," February 14, 1949, Social Security folder 2, Charles Murphy papers (Harry S. Truman Library, Independence, Mo.).

36. Arthur Altmeyer interview by Peter Corning, 1966, pp. 122–23, Columbia Oral History Collection (Columbia University, New York).

37. Blanche D. Coll's work (see her "Public Assistance: Reviving the Original Comprehensive Concept of Social Security," to be published in *Social Security: The First Half Century*) offers an essential supplement and corrective.

38. See Theda Skocpol and John Ikenberry, "The Political Formation of the American Welfare State in Historical and Comparative Perspective," in Richard Tomasson, ed., *Comparative Social Research* 6 (1983), pp. 124–25.

39. Edward D. Berkowitz, "The First Social Security Crisis," *Prologue* 15 (Fall 1983), pp. 133–49.

40. Cates, *Insuring Inequality*, p. 72.

41. See, for example, Lenore Epstein, "Money Income Position of the Aged, 1948–1955" *Social Security Bulletin* 19 (April 1956), pp. 7–14; Bill File on H.R. 6000, 81st Congress, Records of the Senate Committee on Finance, Record Group 46 (National Archives, Washington, D.C.).

42. Skocpol and Ikenberry, "Political Formation," pp. 188–89.

43. Hugh Heclo, *Modern Social Policies in Britain and Sweden* (New Haven: Yale University Press, 1974).

44. Weaver, *Crisis in Social Security*, pp. 124, 143.

45. Derthick, *Policymaking for Social Security*, p. 207; for incrementalism see in particular p. 26.

46. Mark Leff, "Taxing the 'Forgotten Man': The Politics of Social Security Finance in the New Deal," *Journal of American History* 70 (September 1983), pp. 359–81.

47. See Edward Berkowitz, "History, Public Policy and Reality," *Journal of Social History* 18 (Fall 1984), p. 81.

48. See Clarke A. Chambers, "Social Reform, Social Work, and Social Security: A Subject Revisited," in Schacht, ed., *The Quest for Security*, pp. 1–17.

49. See in particular W. Andrew Achenbaum, *Social Security: Visions and Revisions* (New York: Cambridge University Press, forthcoming).

# 3

# The First Advisory Council and the 1939 Amendments

## EDWARD D. BERKOWITZ

As Mark Leff has demonstrated, social security has passed through at least three phases: from controversy in the period between 1935 to 1950, to a golden age of expansion and acceptance from 1950 to 1972, to a period of financial crisis and renewed controversy in the years from 1972 to the present. If one had inquired into the status of social security in 1982 and 1983, one would have discovered considerable turmoil. Newspapers and other periodicals carried alarming stories. *USA Today*, with its eye-catching graphics and colorful first page, warned that the "Old Age Fund Could Go Bust in July" and that every day the "System Goes 65M Deeper in Hole." Less sensational publications ran similar stories. "To put the matter bluntly," wrote Peter Peterson in the *New York Review of Books*, a journal not noted for plain speaking, "social security is headed for a crash."[1]

Responding to the threat of a crash, President Ronald Reagan appointed a bipartisan commission. Throughout 1982, the commission endeavored to patch up the damage done to the system by a recession that reduced the amount paid into the system through payroll taxes and increased the amount paid out through benefits that rose with the inflation rate.

The discussions of this commission, as with all official discussions of social security, were cast in highly technical terms. White House officials and U.S. senators listened to actuaries and economists lecture on bend points, replacement ratios, and cost-of-living adjustments. They translated what they heard into the cost-benefit ratios of politics. Then, in an impressive demonstration of respect for the program, key actors on the commission fashioned a political compromise that would, it appeared, keep the program solvent into the next century. Each side sacrificed something. The Democrats, led by such respected social security figures as Robert Ball, agreed to such things as a one-time omission of the cost-of-living adjustment. The Republicans, led by such important political actors as David Stockman and Robert Dole, acquiesced to increased social security taxes. All of these individuals would have been the first to admit that problems remained. Early in the next century begins the difficult period when the retirement of the baby boom will strain the pay-as-you-go system. Although the commissioners understood the magnitude of the problem, they were also public officials who took as their responsibility responding to the political problems of the moment. They opted for an honorable way out of the immediate crisis.[2]

In this regard, the modern crisis in social security resembled the earlier one that began in 1935. This first social security crisis lasted for four years and ended with the passage of the 1939 amendments to the Social Security Act. Having solved some of the political problems of social security, Congress then largely put it aside, debating only the extension of coverage and the expansion of the program to cover new risks such as hospital care and disability. It was not until the recent economic crisis that social security was thrust back into politics. By then, of course, few remembered the first social security crisis and the first social security commission.

As the preceding and following chapters remind us, social security did not instantly become a venerated institution. The act required collection of 1 percent of the first $3,000 of each employee's earnings, to be matched by 1 percent from his employer. This provision went into effect in January 1937. Payments of benefits were not scheduled to begin until 1942. From 1937 to 1942, therefore, a part of each employee's paycheck went into the treasury, not into any retired person's pocket. For the years before payments began, social security endured a period of political peril, collecting people's money and offering little more than promises in return.

Adding to the instability, the routines of social security were far from settled. Things that Americans now take for granted still needed to be invented and tested against experience. In May 1938, for example, social security officials met with a group of employers who questioned the point of providing workers with receipts for social security deductions. Most workers, the employers said, simply threw the receipts away. Suspicious employees wanted to go to the social security records office in Baltimore and make sure that their contributions had been credited to their accounts.[3]

What would those workers find in Baltimore? Few Americans knew for sure. The politics of 1935 had already made the financing mechanisms of social security very complex. In 1935, President Roosevelt objected to a system that would take money from general revenues to pay for social security. Instead, he wanted a system that financed social security benefits from money collected through payroll taxes. Although many of the president's advisors disagreed with him on this point, they followed his orders and designed a system that fulfilled his wishes.[4]

The president's desire to keep the system self-financing made it more complex to explain than it otherwise would have been. Under any method of financing, the obligations of social security would increase as time passed. In 1980, after all, a much larger percentage of the retired population would have contributed to the program than in 1942. Most of the retired population would be excluded from receiving benefits in 1942 since so many of them would not have contributed to the social security system. Therefore, it would take more money to sustain the system in 1980 than in 1942; actuaries estimated that as much as 10 percent of the nation's payroll might be required in 1980. Under the president's plan, this money would come from payroll taxes that would eventually reach 6 percent of "covered" or "taxable" payroll and from interest earnings on money that had been set aside in the early years of the plan when benefit payments would be relatively low. The alternative plan, which the president had rejected, called for adding general revenues to the social security taxes.

"The problem is so complex that the ordinary citizen can't understand its full implications and that probably is its greatest weakness," Arthur Altmeyer, the head of the Social Security Board which administered the program, wrote. "The plan is sound but not simple."[5] No, indeed, the plan was not simple. Employers and employees paid taxes; employers sent the tax money to the Treasury Department, which put the money into the same pile as all of the other money it received. The money from social security taxes was not legally dedicated to social security (and would not be until 1939). Instead, Congress needed to appropriate the money into the social security account. Once in the social security account, the money was used to pay benefits. The money that was left over, a considerable amount in the early years of the plan, was invested in special government securities. In future years, the interest on those securities would keep the social security system solvent; in the meantime, the Treasury Department used the money it raised through the sale of the securities just as it would any other money it received.

The amount of money involved in these transactions reached extraordinary levels. In 1937, Congress appropriated $511 million to the social security account, only $6 million of which was required for current expenses. In 1937, therefore, most of the social security money went into what government officials called the "reserve account." In 1967, with the system much farther along the road to maturity, the appropriation would be more than $2 billion. For the first time, however, benefits would cost more than the appropriation, and money from the interest on the more than $38 billion that had accumulated in the reserve account would make up the difference. At the far end of the actuaries' calculations, in 1980, appropriations would reach more than $2 billion and benefits more than $3.5 billion. By this time, however, the balance on the reserve would have reached over $46 billion. The system, although highly complex and subject to the vagaries of demography and the economy, provided a means of stockpiling payroll taxes to cover the future debts of the system.[6]

Criticism of the reserve plan began almost as soon as its details were announced. The Republicans, starved for a winning issue, decided to turn the criticisms to their advantage. They charged that the 1935 act was financially unworkable. Succumbing to inflammatory rhetoric, they stated in their 1936 platform, "The so-called reserve fund estimated at $47,000,000,000 is no reserve at all, because the fund will contain nothing but the government's promise to pay, while the taxes collected in the guise of premiums will be wasted in reckless and extravagant political schemes."[7]

On September 26, 1936, presidential candidate Alfred Landon gave a speech that would cause him political difficulty for the rest of his life. In the spirit of his party's platform, he blasted social security as "unjust, unworkable, stupidly drafted and wastefully financed." He underscored the fact that no benefits would be paid until 1942, and, even then, no benefits would be paid to a worker's wife and children. He reserved the brunt of his scorn for the financing provisions of the bill. "We have some good spenders in Washington," he said. "With this social security money alone running into billions of dollars, all restraint on Congress will be off."[8]

In attacking social security, Landon took a position that was far from isolated or extreme. In the late thirties, the Brookings Institution, the American Federation of Labor, the Chamber of Commerce, the heads of most insurance companies, and the editorial board of the *New York Times* concurred with Landon's judgment. They all agreed that the financing plan of social security amounted, in the words of the *New York Times*, to "financial hocus pocus." As journalist Mark Sullivan explained to his readers, social security taxes went into the Treasury's general fund. "From that fund they may be spent for any legal purpose under the sun and in practice they are now being used to help the Government's current bills— perhaps to build the Grand Coulee Dam, perhaps to finance WPA projects in street paving, perhaps to pay the salaries of officers in the Navy." Altmeyer, as head of the Social Security Board, routinely received correspondence of the sort that told him, "Criticism of the accumulation and disposition of reserves is mounting rapidly."[9]

Although the election of 1936 produced a Democratic landslide, the Republicans refused to let go of the social security issue. It continued to serve as an excellent means of using the New Deal as a weapon against itself. The issue united those who wanted old-age pensions without payroll taxes and those who believed in prudent management of the government's money. Radicals and conservatives, funny money men and hard currency supporters, all joined in condemning social security, using Republican party politics as a sounding board.

On January 29, 1937, Senator Arthur Vandenberg (R–Mich.) offered Resolution 4 to his colleagues. Vandenberg dismissed the contemplated method of financing social security, a method responsible for the paycheck deductions that had just begun, as a needless "fiscal and economic menace." He recommended instead that benefits should begin sooner, that initial benefits be higher, and that the social security tax increase scheduled for 1940 be postponed. These actions pointed the way toward what Vandenberg called a "reasonable contingency reserve."

According to Vandenberg and three of his Republican colleagues, the piling up of the huge reserve constituted "a positive menace to free institutions and sound finance" and a "perpetual invitation to the maintenance of an extravagant public debt." Those least able to pay the taxes—wage earners making less than $3,000 a year—bore the brunt of the tax. They contributed a higher percentage of their total income than did the rich, and they also faced the threat of laying out more of their money for staple goods should employers pass along the costs to consumers. If one relied instead on a pay-as-you-go scheme, with the money taken from general revenues, then these regressive taxes would no longer be necessary, benefits could begin immediately, and the need for a large reserve would cease.[10]

The size of the contemplated reserve proved an irresistible target because it revealed in stark relief the implications of a federal program that reached over half of the American population. In a labor force of about 49 million workers, social security promised to pay old-age benefits to nearly 27.5 million of them. Even modest pensions paid to such a large number of workers amounted to sums of money that dwarfed previous federal spending efforts in peacetime. To have $47 billion held in reserve for such a program staggered the American imagination. The figure represented eight times the amount of money then in circulation in the United States, nearly five times the amount of money in savings banks—enough money to buy all the farms in the United States, with $14 billion to spare. "Such a treasure—all in one place and conveniently eligible for Congressional raids through the years—is an utterly naive conception," wrote Vandenberg. "That it would remain intact and not suffer periodical depletions is more than human nature in a political democracy can rationally anticipate."[11]

Altmeyer faced the formal responsibility of responding to Vandenberg during a February 1937 hearing of the Senate Committee on Finance. Altmeyer noted that shifting costs to general revenues put the million of self-employed and agricultural workers, who were not covered by social security, at a great disadvantage. He explained that, without a reserve, tax rates after 1949 would need to increase from 6 percent to 10 percent. Senator Vandenberg persisted in questioning Altmeyer about how the reserve fund worked. At the end of the hearing, Vandenberg asked Altmeyer if he would object to a congressional commission inquiring into the matter. Altmeyer had little choice but to agree.[12]

The Social Security Board dragged its feet on the advisory commission through the spring and into the summer of 1937; then Altmeyer and his colleagues began to see a way out of the dilemma. In September, Altmeyer wrote a memorandum to the president and told him that the council provided the administration with the means of putting concern over the reserve to rest in a desirable way. "I think," he wrote, "it is possible not only to offset the attacks on the Social Security Act but really to utilize them to advance a socially desirable program." He thought it best to "go off the reserve with our eyes open" and increase benefits without lowering taxes. By October 1937, a month before the advisory council's first meeting, this strategy became the accepted one of the Social Security Board.[13]

With the basic strategy agreed upon, Altmeyer greeted the advisory council on November 5, 1937. The council contained twenty-five members who had been chosen by the Social Security Board and the Senate Committee on Finance. Six of the members represented labor, six sat as representatives of management, and thirteen were appointed to serve the interests of the "general public." When Arthur Altmeyer spoke to the group, he emphasized that the Social Security Act was not a "finished product," that it could bear some "extending and improving." For the next thirteen months, the employees of the Social Security Board served as mentors to the members of the advisory council, leading them on a course that would substantially alter the Social Security Act.[14]

The course of training began with a strenuous set of lectures on such topics as financing, extending coverage, and beginning benefits before 1942.[15] Despite the daunting nature of the topics, the discussions became quite lively. The sessions on extending coverage, for example, turned into seminars on the behavior of the American work force. The group ripe for expansion was the self-employed—the small businessman who worked on his own, tending a store or farm; the casual laborer who mowed lawns, cleaned houses, or picked fruit. In discussing these groups, the advisory council tended to indulge in racial and other stereotypes. Domestic workers, for example, were personified by the "colored woman . . . who goes from house to house for a day's work here and a day's work there." She had too many employers to keep track of and could not be trusted to remember them all. Farmers, not noted for their business acumen, lacked the capability to keep records; some paid their employees in kind, not cash. As for four-and-a-half million "storekeepers" or "peanut vendors," they would have to contribute both the employee and employer shares, a double tax burden. To weigh down these employers with such taxes violated the American image of free enterprise.[16]

As the abstract discussions on basic principles proceeded during the November and December 1937 meetings, representatives of business, labor, and other interests found spokesmen and staked out their political positions. The chief adversaries on the council were Edwin Witte, an economist from the University of Wisconsin, former executive director of the Committee on Economic Security, and a strong defender of the existing social security law, and W. Albert Linton, an actuary and insurance executive, who saw disaster in the way that the law was financed. More than any other individual, Witte helped to create the Social Security Act of 1935. Now, in the face of criticism of his work, he asked that the act be given a trial before Congress made major changes. In particular, he objected to a system funded from general revenues. Not only did such a system fail to reward individual effort, but also it raised the possibility that no money would be appropriated for future generations.[17] Linton disagreed. He objected strenuously to any system that required the government to hold large reserves. He said that $47 billion represented too much of a temptation. Instead of letting the reserve accumulate, Congress would make benefits more liberal and leave a crushing burden for the future. "I think we are going to come to 1980 without the help of the reserve fund and we are going to be faced with the benefits of 9 1/2% of payroll and none of these helps to bear the load," Linton concluded.[18]

Witte and Linton engaged in an argument that made sense only in the context of social security. Witte, a liberal and a friend of the Roosevelt administration, wanted to use conservative means to protect liberal ends; Linton exactly reversed the process. Witte wanted to preserve the notion of people paying into an insurance fund; Linton, an insurance executive, preferred to drop the insurance analogy and move, at least partially, to a pay-as-you-go scheme funded from general revenues.

Witte and Linton's argument concerned the future. Others on the council, such as the labor representatives, based their reasoning squarely on current events. The labor representatives attended meetings on a sporadic basis, a fact which exasperated Witte and Altmeyer. When Philip Murray of the CIO appeared at the November meeting, he spoke in terms far different from the social security experts. He suggested that money from payroll taxes be spent on public housing and other construction. In this manner, he united the future plans of the social insurance experts and the current concerns of the labor movement for jobs. The building industry was so fundamental to the economy that money spent on it would ripple through the entire economy. To Linton this suggestion represented his fears for the worst. He objected vehemently to using social security funds to "finance socialistic schemes."[19]

Unlike Linton, officials of the Social Security Board sympathized with Murray's suggestion and even had taken steps in private to act upon it. Exasperated by the constant criticism of social security, Altmeyer contacted Senator Robert Wagner (D–N.Y.) and offered the tentative suggestion of using reserve funds for public housing. "One way in which perhaps much of the criticism might be allayed," Altmeyer reasoned, "would be to invest the funds in enterprises which in themselves promote social security." Wilbur Cohen, who served as Altmeyer's assistant, made the same argument to Benjamin Cohen of the White House staff. Low-cost housing and slum clearance legislation all fell under the domain of a "larger program of social security."[20]

Cohen anticipated a criticism of social security from the left made by the followers of John Maynard Keynes. Social security, according to Harvard economist and advisory council member Alvin Hansen, played havoc with the nation's economy. During a recession, social security taxes continued to be collected. That increased the government's revenues and took money out of circulation, just when the Keynesian approach to economic management called for exactly the opposite. As Hansen expressed this idea to Altmeyer, "Every time we face a tendency toward recession the impounding of this Old Age Reserve Account will plague us and add to our difficulties in overcoming a recession." A better approach was to begin paying benefits sooner and have the amount collected in taxes equal the amount paid in benefits. When the load got onerous, around 1960, government contributions could be added to payroll taxes. Altmeyer agreed that the "effect of this reserve on the business cycle is important," but argued that the money collected did not lie idle. It returned to the public in the form of Works Progress Administration payments and other public expenditures.[21]

Early in 1938, both Altmeyer's organization and the advisory council began to put some distance between themselves and the solidly condemned reserve financing plan. Douglas Brown, a Princeton labor economist who had agreed to chair the advisory council, served as a messenger boy who brought the work of the actuaries and other social security planners to the advisory council and as a referee who kept the opposing factions from deadlocking the council. In February 1938, he reported solid progress in creating a new, compromise plan that might overcome everyone's objections and gain the acceptance of Congress as well.

Brown began the council's February meeting with a note of reassurance. He and Linton had visited the social security records office in Baltimore. Having seen the future, Brown and Linton decided that it worked. "We were tremendously impressed with the efficiency and the complexity, but at the same time the simplicity . . . of the operation," Brown said. After hearing so much criticism of the Social Security Board's operations, Brown told the council that his visit to Baltimore was "very much a breath of fresh air." The social security employees won over the stern and exacting Linton by leading him to his account and finding his name and address from among the more than 26 million names in the records. "I think it is amazing," Linton said, "the way they have solved the technical aspect of this from the Washington end." The social security operations were, in fact, amazing. During 1937, for example, the staff processed 75.1 million pieces of information concerning employees' earnings and established 40 million account numbers.[22]

Even as Brown allayed the council members' fears over the administrative mechanisms of social security, he proposed to make substantive changes in the nature and content of social security. He calmly presented Advisory Council Plan One (Plan AC–1) and commended it to the council as a plan "worth considering." Stripped of bureaucratic and insurance jargon, Plan AC–1 introduced a benefit for a man's wife and another benefit for a man's widow. A married family received one and one-half times the amount of a single man; a widow of a social security beneficiary got three-quarters of a man's benefit. Here, then, was the first divergence from the relatively simple system created in 1935, one that made no distinction between single and married workers, with no special provisions, beyond a lump-sum payment to the dead man's estate, for widows. This divergence eased part of the reserve problem by increasing the level of benefits and, therefore, not creating quite as large a reserve.[23]

Most advisory council members reacted with enthusiasm to this tacit retreat from the reserve plan. The significant exception was Marion Folsom, the treasurer of the Eastman Kodak Company and a spokesman for the other businessmen on the council. Folsom said that the wife and widow benefits represented too much of an expansion of social security too early in the program's life. "I think we are trying to get across in two or three years what other countries have taken 30 and 35 years to do," he argued. Folsom claimed that if he were an administrator of the act, "I would hate to have the additional things thrown at me until I had licked the things in the present act."[24]

Although overextending the social security system concerned Folsom, not everyone came out a winner under the terms of Plan AC–1. Married men gained an advantage over single men. Under the existing law, a single man with thirty-five years of coverage and an average wage of $50 a month stood to get $30 a month from social security. Under the terms of Plan AC–1, this same man would receive only $27.50 a month; if he were married, his benefit would increase to $41.25.[25]

As these numbers revealed, the advisory council faced decisions that were as much social as economic. It cost more for married people to live than for a single person; therefore, married people deserved more than a single person. The logic of this argument depended on a social observation and nothing else. In succumbing to this logic, the advisory council took the social security system away from what might be called a "pure insurance" model in which benefits were determined by contributions or "premiums." Now, planners extended the design of the original plan and elevated social adequacy above individual equity. Although the original act provided a greater return to poorer and recent contributors than to richer and longer-term contributors, it did not discriminate among people with the same employment history. Under the new plan, everyone with the same employment history would not be treated in exactly the same way. Theresa McMahon, a professor at the University of Washington and one of the council members representing the public, expressed this new concept in social security in her usual acerbic manner. "I don't mind taxing the bachelors. I think they ought to take on the responsibility of sharing their income with somebody else."[26]

The decision to favor married workers over single workers proved relatively easy to make. Beyond this simple decision, however, many problems remained. The advisory council and the Social Security Board found themselves in the position of inventing a social welfare system based on the principle of social adequacy, and they made the rules as they went along. In doing so, they mirrored widely held notions about the nature of families, women, and minorities. Plan AC–1, for example, called for a widow's benefit pegged at 75 percent of the basic benefit. Linton wondered why a widow's benefit should be less than a single man's benefit— why not 50 percent or some other arbitrary number? The actuary for the Social Security Board replied that the widow could "look out for herself better than the man could." "Is that a sociological fact?" Linton asked. Brown restated this question in a manner which reflected the sexual stereotypes of the day. "Can a single woman adjust herself to a lower budget on account of the fact that she is used to doing her own housework whereas the single man has to go to a restaurant?" The question was left hanging.[27]

The question of race arose in a similarly oblique fashion during a discussion of lump-sum benefits. The 1935 law had a money-back guarantee; if a worker died before retirement age, his estate received a lump-sum payment equal to 3.5 percent of the wages credited to his account. Reformers had never looked kindly on lump-sum arrangements of this sort because they placed too much temptation in the path of a program's beneficiaries. This view reflected the paternalism that many advisory council members brought to their tasks and implied a very unflattering view of the working class. Advisory council member Walter D. Fuller, president of the company that published the *Saturday Evening Post*, for example, told a cautionary tale of a "colored man in our employ who died. He was a widower and he had two minor children and he left $2,000 insurance. It was turned over to the family, and they immediately tried to run it up in a numbers game and lost it in two weeks."[28]

By the end of the February meeting, the advisory council had gone a long way toward recommending the radical alteration of the social security program. The group decided, with almost no controversy, that benefits should be increased in the early years of the plan, that benefits should be increased by paying more to wives, and that benefits to single people should be reduced to compensate in part for the new benefits.

As the advisory council took these actions in private, social security remained a lively public issue in the spring of 1938. On April 8, for example, Senator Henry Cabot Lodge (R–Mass.) proposed that payroll taxes be cut almost in half. He said that the payroll taxes exacerbated an already bad economic situation. The Senate defeated his proposal, but the incident made Vandenberg all the more impatient to see the advisory council's recommendations. This flurry of politics led to a formal request from President Roosevelt that the advisory council prepare its recommendations in time for the next session of Congress in January.[29]

The politicians, particularly the Republicans, cared little for the intricacies of social security: they wanted to hear something about the financing problem and the $47 billion reserve. Aware that the council owed its existence to this political issue, the members approached it in a cautious and politically partisan manner. The sense of discovery that marked discussions of some topics, such as family coverage, gave way to rote political responses.

The brunt of the work in dealing with the issue fell on Brown and on a special interim committee, a small core group of seven people who tried to facilitate the full council meetings by agreeing on solutions to the major issues in advance. Critics of the administration's policies dominated the interim committee. Witte complained to Altmeyer, "With the labor people invariably absent, the Interim Committee is in control of the anti-administration men." "My view," he continued, is that "the Social Security Advisory Council is a very poor body to work out a revision of the [law]." The attacks on social security were "mainly political—an attempt to further embarrass the Roosevelt Administration."[30]

Altmeyer tended to agree with Witte's characterization of the interim committee as "hopeless." During a critical meeting of the committee in April, not one of the labor members showed up. Brown, Linton, Fuller, and Folsom were the only members in attendance. Although Brown began the meeting by suggesting that a decision on financing be deferred until the payroll tax level reached 4 percent (2 percent each from employers and employees), which it was scheduled to do in 1943, he was, in Altmeyer's words, "swept off his feet." Anxious to avoid any hint of a tax raise and firmly opposed to the reserve method of financing, the businessmen present wanted to adopt a statement condemning the reserve plan and favoring a pay-as-you-go plan. Altmeyer, who described himself as "outspoken in protesting such action," managed to defer the discussion.[31]

Because Altmeyer and Witte feared that opponents of social security would use the wide disapproval of the reserve plan as a means of discrediting the integrity of the entire social security program, they prepared a simple statement on financing. Essentially this statement said that, whatever problems existed in the long run, the government was handling the social security funds it currently received in a proper manner. Witte drafted the statement so that it would "provoke a minimum of discussion when the Council holds its next meeting." Witte conceded that, "if the members of the Council want to play the political game of the anti-administration people, they may vote down the statement but I think they should be smoked out."[32]

Witte need not have worried. The council adopted his reassuring statement on social security financing and released it to Senator Vandenberg and the press. The statement said that the way in which the government handled social security funds "did not involve any misuse of these funds or endanger the safety of these funds."

Such a statement did little to end the debate over social security financing. It said nothing about whether a large reserve should be allowed to develop and whether the government should begin to contribute to the system as a means of supplementing employer and employee contributions. By now, the terms of the debate had begun to shift within the advisory council, as an April 1938 debate between Witte and Folsom revealed. The debate resembled previous financing discussions in that it made sense only within the confines of social security financing and could not easily be translated into a broader political discussion. The debate hinged on whether the federal government should begin contributing to the social security fund immediately, as Witte wanted, or whether the government should wait until the reserves had been spent before it made its contributions, as Folsom wanted. In other words, Witte and Folsom debated the reserve financing question, only this time with government contributions thrown into the discussion. Witte continued to favor the reserve plan or a fully funded system; Folsom favored a pay-as-you-go plan. The council continued to resist either alternative, confining its official statements to the bland endorsement of the government's propriety that Witte and Altmeyer had cooked up.[33]

As the debate over financing proceeded, the council members proved capable of discarding their political personae and endorsing a major change in the design of social security with only the slightest hesitation. During the April 1938 meeting, Brown unveiled Plan AC-12. Unlike the previous plans, AC-12 contained provisions for benefits to be paid to the dependent children of a deceased worker. Furthermore, these benefits were to be based on a worker's "average" wages. In the original Social Security Act, all benefits were based on the total wages on which taxes were payable, which, in the jargon of social security, were called "credited wages." Plan AC–12 suggested a radical revision of this concept. In order to pay adequate benefits to dependent children, this new type of benefit would more closely reflect what the worker had been making at the time he died. If he had accumulated relatively little in his social security fund because of his youth, the new concept lessened the resulting penalty on his survivors. The move marked another retreat from the concept of equity to that of adequacy. It further reduced the similarity in treatment between two workers with the same wage records. The worker who died and left behind dependent children would get back more on his social security investment than would the worker who lived until old age, never married, and never had children. The move toward survivors benefits also meant that lump-sum death benefits were severely curtailed. Instead, a family received protection based on the concept of social adequacy. A man was entitled to benefits for his wife, for his widow, and now for his dependent children. If a man died after he reached retirement age and left behind no wife or children, his social security payments would simply stop, and his estate would receive nothing. Here again was a shift from equity, the notion of getting back what you paid into the system, to a system that recognized certain social problems as more pressing than others and took steps to solve those problems.[34]

Once on the road to adequacy, it became difficult to know just how far to go. In the late thirties, in the middle of a severe recession that seemed to offer no hope that the depression would ever end, social problems were so numerous and so severe that all of the federal government's money could be spent on solving them without any assurance of success. Social security, for the most part, was irrelevant to considerations of most of these problems since it was not even scheduled to begin paying benefits until four years from the time that the advisory council met. Further, it provided monetary benefits, and no further services, only to the families of retired or dead people who had worked in industrial or commercial pursuits. Even in the limited terms of social security, however, an important gap in coverage remained after the adoption of Plan AC–12, and that proved to be the point at which the advisory council drew the line.

On the road to adequacy, the advisory council stopped at disability. Disability constituted a form of involuntary retirement, and it posed many of the same problems as the early death of the wage earner. It left the family of the wage earner in the same precarious financial position. The logic of adequacy, therefore, demanded that the board include disability in its plans.

Disability presented problems as difficult as any the Social Security Board had ever confronted. Even as the staff worked on plans to present to the advisory council, disputes erupted over the cost of disability protection. One of the actuaries threatened to resign if the advisory council received an inaccurate impression of the "unknown quantity" that was disability insurance. The actuary said that there were "so many variables in the discussion that he could not possibly give one estimate and maintain his personal integrity."[35]

Despite this internal dispute, the Social Security Board presented Plan AC–13, complete with provision for permanent disability insurance, to the council on October 21, 1938. The disgruntled actuary told the council of his fears for disability insurance. "It seems almost inevitable that when men are laid off and cannot work," he said, "with nothing in sight, no earning power whatever, they will be judged disabled." Others on the council pointed to the adverse experience of private insurance companies with disability insurance; they had tried to offer disability protection and had lost their shirts during the depression when unemployed workers pressed disability claims. After listening to the arguments, Council Chairman Brown, who had been very sympathetic to the Social Security Board plans, decided not to endorse disability insurance. In response to an accusation from Lee Pressman of the CIO that Brown lacked social concern, Brown said, "It is very simple. I feel that this whole report is related to cost. To recommend benefits without some understanding of costs is like saying, 'I want an automobile, but I don't want to pay for it.' "[36]

On the matter of disability insurance, the council inched toward a compromise. After a lengthy discussion of the merits of a welfare program to cover disability (as opposed to a social insurance program), the council passed a motion that stated the council agreed that disability insurance was desirable but disagreed on when disability insurance should begin.[37]

The deliberations over disability insurance marked the climax of the advisory council's affairs. The shape of the report, which was issued in December 1938, now became clear. It would recommend survivors benefits for widows and dependent children and a special increase in the basic benefit for wives; it would avoid specific recommendations on financing; and it would advise delay in implementing disability insurance.

It remained only to tighten the recommendations and make them internally consistent. After much soul-searching, for example, the group decided to follow the Social Security Board's lead and to have a wife's benefit and widow's benefit begin at age 65. Altmeyer confessed that no scientific consideration motivated this decision so much as a desire to impose uniformity on the social security system. "We worked for three months on that one problem," he said. "You go from one extreme to the other. You can say that the widows' age shall have to be 65 . . . or you can go to the other extreme and say that widows of any age shall be eligible." Lacking a more objective criterion, the Social Security Board and the advisory council opted for age 65; widows and wives benefits had the resulting virtue of beginning at the same age as old-age benefits.[38]

As the advisory council tied up its recommendations into a neat package, the group agreed to recommend a "reasonable contingency reserve," a concept that Witte described as "something of a fudge factor." The concept, which had originally been used by Senator Vandenberg, meant something different to each of the advisory council members. The only logic behind the recommendation was that it enabled the council to say something without offending any one group. As such it embodied the well-intentioned ambiguity that often lies at the heart of political compromise.[39]

In a sense, the council did a disservice to later generations by giving Congress the impression that benefits could be increased at no cost to the taxpayer. In the short run, that strategy proved correct: benefits could be increased in the early years of a social insurance plan without running into financial difficulties. As the system matured, however, the system would encounter problems, since no money had been set aside to meet the increase in costs that would accompany a large number of retired people who were covered by social security. The council tacitly assumed that the government would make up the difference. Indeed, the council recommended that "the principle of distributing the eventual cost of the old age insurance system by means of approximately equal contributions by employers, employees, and the government is sound." But the council never made any definite suggestions on when the government contributions should begin; the debate that had taken place between Witte and Folsom never was resolved. Congress, for its part, failed to write the principle of government contributions into law until nearly forced to do so in 1983 by just the sort of crisis that council members feared would take place and, even then, in a very indirect manner.

Even at the time of the advisory council report, this failure to come to grips with the financing question drew criticism. As Alanson Wilcox, an employee of the Social Security Board, explained to the council, the suggestions on government contributions were

> meaningless.... There is no such thing as drawing a government contribution out of thin air.... It is likely to have a narcotic effect on the Congressmen.... If Congress once forms the habit of... asking for a raise in benefits and future government contributions, it seems to me that we will have taken off the only real safety valve we have in the program.... We have set the precedent. We have said we can finance this. We have said we can push off into the future the question of where this money comes from.[40]

The members of the advisory council, like everyone else, lacked the ability to predict the future. They felt they handled a politically volatile problem in a responsible way by producing a report that could be transformed into legislation. Proceeding from the council's analysis, the legislative process functioned smoothly. By February 1939, the House of Representatives began hearings on legislation. The Committee on Ways and Means accepted most of the recommendations, rejecting only those that called for major extensions of coverage. As an elderly Robert Doughton, chairman of the committee, explained to Altmeyer, "Doctor, when the first farmer with manure on his boots comes to me and asks to be covered, I will be willing to consider it."[41] Apparently no such farmer soiled the halls of Congress. By June the social security bill was passed by the House and sent to the Senate. In little more than a month, the Senate passed the bill and gave it to the president. The president signed it gladly on August 10, 1939, happy to remove social security from the debit side of the political ledger.

When people want to agree on something, they often overlook the true implications of the thing on which they are agreeing. In such a situation, people tend to excuse other people for abandoning previously held beliefs. In these moments, congressional testimony and debate take on the characteristics of ritual: the compromise requires a person's blessing and not his critical scrutiny. In the case of the Social Security Act Amendments of 1939, the ritual masked points of great historical significance. During the hearings in the House, for example, Secretary of the Treasury Henry Morgenthau backed away from the reserve method of financing that he had insisted on and that had incited so much controversy. He testified that the years in which the Social Security Act had been in operation "throws new light on our original belief that the act ought to be self-supporting." There followed some political sleight of hand.

> The benefits of the act will be so widely diffused that any supplemental funds from general tax revenues may be substituted—without substantial inequity—for a considerable proportion of the expected interest earnings from the large fund contemplated by the present law. Therefore, it becomes apparent that the argument for a large reserve does not have the validity which 4 years ago it seemed to possess.[42]

Only the people at the extremes of the political spectrum tended to see the 1939 amendments as the radical changes that they were. One congressman stated the matter plainly, and accurately, when he said that, "The American people should know that we are now changing the rules in the middle of the game. We are leaving the original principle of individual insurance and individual savings accounts—for a program of social insurance."[43]

And so the crisis ended, much as the crisis of the early eighties did, with the acceptance of a political compromise that was worked out by an advisory commission. The Roosevelt administration abandoned the reserve method of financing in return for a vague promise that government revenues would enter the system sometime in the future. The Republicans surrendered the issue to the Democrats and accepted a social security program that paid more complete and more liberal benefits than the original one. The balance between contributions and expenditures was decisively altered, and the system tilted closer to adequacy than to equity.

The 1939 amendments changed the nature of social security. The discipline of the "insurance approach" to social insurance gave way to a more pragmatic program that balanced social needs against available funds. We live today with the consequences of the 1939 amendments, both in terms of its judgments about the family and in terms of the legacy of pay-as-you-go financing, just as future generations will cope with the consequences of the 1983 amendments. For the political system, after all, there is no long run, only crises that can no longer be avoided. We legislate for tomorrow on the basis of our perceptions of today.

If nothing else, the period between 1935 and 1939 underscores the political difficulties of reserve financing, a fact that should not be neglected by policymakers who will cope with the projected surplus in the coming decades. This period also reminds us that social security was not an inevitable triumph. It did not emerge as a full-grown sacred cow. Instead, its contents were gradually shaped in response to the perceived social needs of the country and the political sentiments prevailing in Congress. The program faced critical choices in the early years of its development, and its response, as codified in the 1939 amendments, gave the program the flexibility that it would need to grow into a major American social welfare program, as well as an inflexibility that would make it so resistant to fundamental change.

## NOTES

1. This chapter is based on an article which appeared in *Prologue* 15 (Fall 1983), pp. 133–49. The editor is grateful to *Prologue* for permission to reprint the essay here. When the essay was originally written, the 1983 amendments had not been passed. This essay updates the original version to reflect the 1983 amendments and other recent developments in social security. *USA Today*, January 14, 1983 and Peterson quoted in Bob Kuttner, "The Social Security Hysteria," *New Republic* (December 27, 1982), p. 17.

2. For more on the 1983 amendments see W. Andrew Achenbaum, *Social Security: Visions and Revisions* (New York: Cambridge University Press, 1986), chap. four; and Paul Light, *Artful Work* (New York: Random House, 1985). For a sober statement on the future of social security,

see Committee for Economic Development, *Reforming Retirement Policies: A Statement by the Research and Policy Committee of the Committee for Economic Development* (1981).

3. John J. Corson to Altmeyer, May 16, 1938, Chairman's Files, Business Advisory Council File, Records of the Social Security Administration, Record Group 47, National Archives (hereafter RG 47).

4. Edwin Witte, *The Development of the Social Security Act* (Madison: University of Wisconsin Press, 1963), p. 74.

5. Altmeyer to Jay Iglauer, November 15, 1937, File 025, RG 47.

6. "Cumulative Tax Collections, Benefit Payments, Net Excess of Tax Collections," (n.d.) and "Annual Appropriations, Benefit Payments and Reserves," (n.d.), File 025, RG 47.

7. Theron F. Schlabach, *Edwin E. Witte: Cautious Reformer* (Madison: Wisconsin State Historical Society, 1969), pp. 158–59; Carolyn Weaver, "The Political Economy of the Emergence and Growth of Social Security," unpublished manuscript, pp. 6.9–6.10.

8. "Text of Governor Landon's Milwaukee Address on Economic Security," *New York Times*, September 26, 1936, p. 31; and Arthur Altmeyer, *The Formative Years of Social Security* (Madison: University of Wisconsin Press, 1966), p. 68.

9. Altmeyer to Secretary Frances Perkins, May 9, 1935, Chairman's Files, Business Advisory Council File, RG 47; Mark Sullivan, "Security or Income Taxes," *Washington Star*, November 1937 in File 705, Old Age Reserve, 1937, Chairman's Files, RG 47; Paul Mellon, "News Behind the News," *Cleveland Plain Dealer*, February 28, 1938; "The Reserve Fund," *New York Times*, September 5, 1938, p. 14; and Iglauer to Brown, March 7, 1938, File 025, RG 47.

10. U.S., Congress, Senate, *Congressional Record*, 75th Congress, 1st Session, January 29, 1937, p. 548.

11. U.S., Congress, Senate, *Congressional Record*, 75th Congress, 1st Session, March 17, 1937, p. 2324; "Composition of Gainful Workers in 1930 with Reference to Coverage Under Old-Age Insurance," File 025, RG 47; Weaver, "Political Economy," p. 6.18.

12. U.S., Congress, Senate, Committee on Finance, *Reserves Under Federal Old-Age Benefit Plan—Social Security Act*, Hearings on S. Con. Res. 4, 75th Congress, 1st Session, February 22, 1937; Altmeyer, *Formative Years*, pp. 88–89.

13. Altmeyer, *Formative Years*, pp. 90, 295–96; Eleanor Lansing Dulles to Ewan Clague, October 23, 1937, File 705, RG 47.

14. Altmeyer, Advisory Council Minutes, November 5, 1937, p. 3, morning session, Chairman's Files, File 025, RG 47. The terms advisory council and advisory commission are used interchangeably here, as they

are in the records. The Advisory Council minutes are verbatim transcripts of the council's meetings.

15. Eleanor Lansing Dulles, *Chances of a Lifetime: A Memoir* (New York: Random House, 1980), p. 153.

16. Presentation of Ewan Clague, Advisory Council Minutes, pp. 8–9, 23, Chairman's Files, RG 47.

17. Edwin Witte, Advisory Council Minutes, November 6, 1937, morning session, pp. 18–19, 24, RG 47; Schlabach, *Cautious Reformer*, p. 164.

18. Schlabach, *Cautious Reformer*, p. 164; Albert Linton, Advisory Council Minutes, November 6, 1937, afternoon session, pp. 12–13, 27, RG 47.

19. Presentation of Philip Murray, Advisory Council Minutes, November 6, 1937, morning session, pp. 13–16, RG 47.

20. Altmeyer to Senator Robert Wagner, February 15, 1937, Wilbur Cohen to Benjamin Cohen, February 15, 1937, File 705, RG 47; Wilbur Cohen to Governor Winant, February 19, 1937, File 025, RG 47.

21. Hansen, Advisory Council Minutes, November 6, 1937, afternoon session, p. 16; Hansen to Altmeyer, November 8, 1937 and Altmeyer to Hansen, December 7, 1937, File 025, RG 47.

22. Brown and Linton, Advisory Council Minutes, February 18, 1938, morning session, p. 2, RG 47.

23. Brown, Advisory Council Minutes, February 18, 1938, morning session, p. 6, RG 47; "Summary of Provisions of Present Title II and Proposed AC–1," (n.d.) and "Reserves at End of Year, Proposed Plan AC–1," (n.d.), RG 47.

24. Folsom, Advisory Council Minutes, February 18, 1938, afternoon session, pp. 35–36, RG 47.

25. "Average Monthly Annuities Under Proposed Plan AC–1 and Under Present Title II, 1940 to 1980," (n.d.) and "Illustrated Monthly Annuities Under Plan AC–1," (n.d.), RG 47.

26. Theresa McMahon, Advisory Council Minutes, February 18, 1938, morning session, pp. 41–42, RG 47.

27. Colloquy among Linton, W. R. Williamson, and Brown, Advisory Council Minutes, February 18, 1938, afternoon session, p. 12, RG 47.

28. Walter Fuller, Advisory Council Minutes, February 18, 1938, afternoon session, p. 34, RG 47.

29. U.S. Congress, Senate, *Congressional Record*, 75th Congress, 2d Session, April 8, 1938, p. 5050; Roosevelt to Altmeyer, April 28, 1938, File 025, RG 47.

30. Witte to Altmeyer, April 2, 1938, RG 47.

31. Altmeyer to Witte, April 8, 1938, RG 47.

32. Witte to Altmeyer, April 12, 1938, Witte to Altmeyer, April 23, 1938, Witte to Altmeyer, April 27, 1938, RG 47.

33. Discussion between Witte and Folsom, Advisory Council Minutes, April 29, 1938, afternoon session, pp. 10–12, RG 47.

34. Brown, Advisory Council Minutes, April 29, 1938, morning session, pp. 17–19, RG 47; "Description of Proposed Plan AC–12," (n.d.), RG 47.

35. Cohen to Altmeyer, October 13, 1938, File 025, RG 47.

36. Williamson, Advisory Council Minutes, October 21, 1938, afternoon session, p. 59, RG 47; Douglas Brown, Advisory Council Minutes, December 10, 1938, morning session, p. 37, RG 47. I discuss disability insurance at much greater length in "The American Disability System in Historical Perspective," in E. Berkowitz, ed., *Disability Policies and Government Programs* (New York: Praeger Press, 1979), pp. 16–74; Edward Berkowitz and Kim McQuaid, *Creating the Welfare State* (New York: Praeger Press, 1980); and in my forthcoming Twentieth Century Fund study of public policy toward disability.

37. See Witte to Altmeyer, December 16, 1938, RG 47.

38. Altmeyer, Advisory Council Minutes, October 21, 1938, morning session, p. 57, RG 47.

39. Witte, Advisory Council Minutes, October 22, 1938, morning session, p. 52, RG 47.

40. Mr. Wilcox, Advisory Council Minutes, October 22, 1938, morning session, p. 74, RG 47.

41. Altmeyer, *Formative Years*, p. 99.

42. "Statement of Secretary of Treasury Morgenthau before Ways and Means," Friday, March 24, 1939, File 705, RG 47.

43. See U.S. Congress, House, *Congressional Record*, 76th Congress, 1st Session, June 8, 1939, p. 6861.

# 4

# Social Security and the Economists

## HENRY J. AARON AND LAWRENCE H. THOMPSON

Changes in the attitudes of American economists toward the U.S. social security program resemble the reported attitudes of English upper-class parents toward their maturing offspring. When the social security system was in its infancy, economists regarded it with great interest and affection. They ignored the institution during its childhood. As social security reached maturity, economists reacted with a mixture of embarrassment and shock.

One might expect such a transformation in attitude to be traceable to some combination of changes in economic analysis and amendments to social security. In fact, however, the basic elements of social security have changed little since the late 1930s, and, although social security has received sharp criticism over the past decade from economists and others, these critics appear to have had little influence on public attitudes and public policy.

Public opinion polls and the behavior of the Congress suggest that social security is unique among government programs in the breadth and depth of its support. Even those who profess a lack of confidence in their own future benefits seem to favor continuing the program at roughly its present scale. Perhaps, as the critics believe, the American public will one day realize the folly of the current arrangement and provide the political support necessary

to achieve major reform; perhaps the analyses of the critics will
be found deficient.

Over the years, the concerns of economists with social security
have changed more than the program itself. Initially, economists
concentrated on the adequacy of benefits, the effect of the program
on labor supply, the source of program revenues, and the level of
reserves. In the 1970s, attention shifted from absolute benefit levels
to the structure of benefits and the implicit returns on workers'
payroll tax contributions. Economists continued to study labor
supply effects and scrutinize program revenue sources. They also
developed an interest in the effect of social security on the savings
rate. Meanwhile, their concern with reserves waned, except as they
affected the savings debate.

In recent years, however, the size of both reserves and benefits
has again become a subject of debate. Renewed interest in reserves
has been sparked by the rapid growth of trust funds projected from
1987 until about 2015 and the subsequent rapid depletion of those
funds. Renewed interest in benefits relates to talk of a coming
generational war, triggered perhaps by projections of increased
costs for social security or by the concern that recent federal budget
cuts have fallen more harshly on children's programs than on benefits for the aged.

This chapter reviews the attitudes of economists toward social
security in three time periods: the 1930s and 1940s, the 1970s and
early 1980s, and today. Not an exhaustive compilation of the economic literature on social security, the chapter highlights changes
in styles and conclusions of economic analyses. It concludes with
some speculations on current issues in the literature, in particular
the economic effects of funding the retirement of the baby boom
generation.[1]

## CREATION OF THE INSTITUTION AND DEBATE OVER
## FINANCING: THE 1930s AND 1940s

The Committee on Economic Security developed what became
the Social Security Act of 1935 in the last six months of 1934.
Congress debated and passed the legislation between January and
August of 1935. This schedule left little time for leisurely analysis
and sober reflection. Moreover, old-age insurance constituted only

one part of the law and, in the eyes of many contemporary observers, not the most important part. As Mark Leff notes in chapter 2, monthly benefits were not scheduled to begin until 1942. Public assistance and unemployment compensation, for which benefits would begin much sooner, appeared to be more pressing concerns.

Not until the initiation of the many other programs created by the 1935 act did Congress turn to the question of old-age insurance. In 1937, as chapter 3 reports, the Senate Finance Committee and the Social Security Board jointly created a blue ribbon advisory panel that included some of the nation's leading economists. As a result, the economics profession probably influenced the program more at this time than at any time since.

One panel member, Alvin Hansen of Harvard, was then serving as president of the American Economic Association (AEA), and two other members, Paul Douglas of the University of Chicago (and later a United States senator from Illinois) and Edwin Witte of the University of Wisconsin, later became AEA presidents. Panel chairman J. Douglas Brown taught economics and industrial relations at Princeton; William Haber belonged to the economics faculty at the University of Michigan. Most of these economists continued to support strongly the institution they helped to shape; several wrote books and papers that explained, analyzed, and defended the system.[2]

The recommendations of the 1937–1938 advisory council formed the basis for major modifications to social security adopted in 1939, which, in turn, created the basic elements of the program as we now know it. The structure of benefits and revenues has changed very little since then.

Many of today's critics allege, however, that beginning in 1950, amendments significantly expanded the social security system enacted in 1935 and modified in 1939. These amendments, it is claimed, converted social security from a program intended to supplement other retirement income into one that provides the majority of retirement income to a large fraction of beneficiaries. (Holders of this view rarely specify the source of this other retirement income that was supposed to be supplemented in 1935.)

Although this view has little merit as stated, it does have some validity if a later period is used as the basis of comparison. Nominal benefit rates under social security were not changed between 1939 and 1950. By 1950, inflation had reduced the ratio of benefits to prevailing wages to a level well below that projected in 1939. Benefit increases in the late 1960s and early 1970s restored the ratio to the level anticipated in the 1935 and 1939 acts. In addition, the payroll tax rate actually needed to finance social security benefits in the 1980s is very similar to the 1980 rate calculated in projections developed in the 1930s. In fact, the ratio of actual 1980 retirement and survivors insurance benefit payments was only one-tenth of 1 percent higher than shown in the official 1938 projections of the 1980 cost. Note, however, that the additional costs of disability and hospital insurance are not included in this comparison, since these programs were added in 1956 and 1965, respectively.[3]

In the 1930s congressional concerns centered on the size of the social security reserve. As reported in detail in the previous chapter, the 1935 act called for payroll taxes to rise to 6 percent (combined employer and employee) by 1949, although projected 1949 benefits could have been financed by a tax rate of only 2 percent (combined). Under the 1935 projections, the reserve continued to grow until about 1970, when it would equal almost twelve times the annual benefit payments. By 1970, however, benefit payments would equal about 9 percent of the taxable payroll; the 6-percent payroll tax would meet two-thirds of the cost, and interest on the accumulated reserve would meet the other third.

As events turned out, however, the 1938 recession quickly followed introduction of the social security payroll tax in 1937. Early followers of Keynes saw a connection between those two events. To increase fiscal stimulus, these economists sought to prevent reserve accumulation by holding social security taxes at rates just sufficient to cover current benefits and administrative costs. Other economists, who wanted to retain the original financing plan, noted that the "reserve" plan could enhance capital formation and permit future payroll taxes to remain one-third lower than would be necessary if reserve accumulation were abandoned.[4]

The Keynesians won. In 1939 Congress approved proposals to abandon accumulation of a large reserve. The 1939 amendments increased benefits in the early years of the program, delayed a payroll tax increase previously scheduled for 1940, and initiated payments two years earlier than scheduled. The changes substantially reduced the projected accumulation. To prevent accidental reserve accumulation, the amendments also required the secretary of the Treasury Department to report if he projected that the fund would exceed three times the highest annual benefit outlay anticipated in the next five fiscal years.

Debate on reserve policy continued throughout the 1940s as Congress repeatedly delayed the effective date of previously scheduled payroll tax increases as it found that the higher taxes were unnecessary to meet current benefit commitments. Proponents of larger reserves continued to lose the debate in the halls of Congress, and the debate eventually ended. Not until 1960 would the combined tax rate reach the 6 percent it had originally been scheduled to reach eleven years earlier.

Martin Feldstein rekindled the controversy in the 1970s when he suggested that large social security reserves be accumulated to enhance national savings.[5] At that time, most economists rejected the Feldstein prescription on the ground that, if higher savings were desirable, better mechanisms than the social security payroll tax could be found to achieve this goal.[6] As the magnitude of retirement costs for the baby boom generation became clear, the issue was again recast, this time in terms of how these burdens should be equitably shared across generations. The 1977 and 1983 amendments called for the accumulation of sizable, although temporary, reserves motivated more by the desire to fund the retirement costs of the baby boom generation in advance than to increase national saving.

## CURRENT FRAMEWORKS FOR ANALYSIS AND EMPIRICAL RESULTS

Disagreements among economists regarding the faults and virtues of social security can usually be traced to the assumptions or model that underlie their analysis. The economists who analyzed social security in the 1930s viewed the institution against the backdrop of an economy experiencing massive market failure. In contrast to the tenets of the classical school, unemployment persisted even as wages fell; banks failed, wiping out a sizable fraction of the private retirement savings that had been accumulated. Economists naturally tended to focus on the effect social security, with its forced savings, promises of future benefits, and incentives to retire, would have on this depressed economy.

Modern economists analyze social security through variants of the neoclassical synthesis. This synthesis holds that if government maintains the proper macroeconomic environment, many of the tenets of the classical school will, in fact, be preserved. The modern view provides a different point of departure for the analysis.

In the approach toward social security today, the first and most important issue concerns how closely actual economic behavior approximates the assumptions of the standard competitive model, the backbone of modern economics. Within this model, markets operate competitively, decisions are rational, and information is widely disseminated and used. In particular, households understand their own wants and have projections of their future resources that cannot be improved upon (or, to be more precise, can be improved only at a cost that exceeds the benefit of the improvement). Based on the information available to them, households decide how much to work and hence to earn and how much to consume and to save.

If one accepts these assumptions, social security can improve household well-being only under special circumstances. If society is saving too much, in the sense that the rate of return to investment is less than the rate of return households demand for deferring consumption, the introduction of pay-as-you-go social security can improve welfare by enabling the current generation to consume more than it could on the basis of its own earnings. It does so by providing benefits to the current generation that are paid for by subsequent generations. If the return to investment is lower than the return savers demand for deferring consumption, the gain to the current generation exceeds the loss to later generations.[7]

Even if these conditions are not satisfied, social security may still improve well-being by providing insurance against risks that private institutions have proven incapable of handling.[8] The most notable "uninsurable" risks flow from the business cycle. Individuals often cannot predict when they will become unemployed. They, therefore, do not know when they might be unable to save for retirement. A rise in aggregate unemployment, particularly a long period of mass unemployment, may upset the long-term plans of many people. These plans, it should be added, may have been rationally conceived for a stable economic environment. No private institution lets people insure against the risk of income loss due to unemployment. Unemployment compensation and old-age insurance effectively do so.

Apart from these special cases, however, the standard economic model suggests that private economic decisions are optimal—or, if not optimal, could be made so through the development of private-market institutions. In such an environment, social security can be no better than innocuous and may well be harmful.

Social security is innocuous if it simply requires people to do what they would have done in its absence or if its requirements can be circumvented without cost. For example, the reduction in current disposable income that results from the payroll tax is an innocuous form of forced savings if people eventually receive benefits that reflect a fair rate of return on those taxes. If a household would have saved at least as much as it is forced to pay in social security taxes, then it can simply reduce its rate of private saving to compensate for social security. As long as the household's return on its social security investment (the taxes it pays for social security) equals the rate of return on private investments for retirement, then retirement income has not changed. In effect, the existence of social security changes nothing.[9] This analysis might even be taken one step further. Even if the household would have saved less than its payroll taxes, social security does no harm—if the household goes to the trouble of borrowing enough money to maintain its present rate of consumption and if that money is available at the same interest rate as the rate of return on the social security taxes.

The two preceding conditions are not satisfied in general, principally because not all households can borrow or lend at the same rate of return as that embodied in the social security system, and some people—those who have decided to consume all of their income and who cannot borrow—may not be able to alter their private saving rate at all.

The key conclusions of economic analysis about the social security system lead to the following syllogism:

Voluntary economic behavior produces optimal results.
Social security distorts voluntary economic decisions.
Therefore, social security reduces welfare.

This characterization may strike some economists as grossly oversimplified. No doubt it is in certain ways. It fails to reveal the elegant and often subtle conclusions about various aspects of economic behavior in general and of social security in particular that can emerge from analyses based on the standard economic model. For example, recent work investigating the degree to which indexation of social security benefits contributes to welfare in a world where households make imperfect forecasts about inflation has concluded that full indexation may reduce welfare. This conclusion rests on the assumptions that savers normally have to give up some yield for greater security and may prefer portfolios with some risk and a higher rate of return. Given the framework of analysis, this finding—that social security reduces welfare—is inescapable.

That leaves only two general rationales for social security. The first is that private institutions are unable to deal with such problems as the unpredictability of unemployment. The second is that the assumptions that underlie the standard economic model are invalid.

The most important of the questionable assumptions is that individuals make rational decisions involving widely separated events and concerning contingencies with low probabilities. For decisions about saving for retirement or for protection against disability to be judged rational, as economists use the term, people must consistently apply the calculus of "expected utility" to uncertain events, and they must understand clearly the wants they will have in the distant future. There is good reason to doubt the realism of both assumptions. A large body of psychological evidence suggests that people underestimate or wholly ignore low-probability events in planning their economic behavior.[10] Such low-probability events include injury or disability at all ages. A large body of literature in economics and management suggests that people may not engage in fully maximizing behavior because of information costs. In such circumstances, otherwise well-functioning markets can produce inferior results.[11] And there is clear evidence drawn from ordinary behavior that people may repeatedly engage in behavior inconsistent with wants they know they will experience in the future.[12] Few people, other than economists, doubt that myopia is widespread in human behavior. The fact that economists are outnumbered on this issue does not prove them wrong; the point is merely that, by making an analytically convenient assumption, they have not proven its validity.

A second flaw in the standard economic model is that it ignores a universal policy in industrial society that causes some people *rationally* to save socially suboptimal amounts for retirement. The universal aversion to letting the indigent starve, expressed through private charity and public assistance, will lead those undeterred by the stigma of accepting such assistance to save less than they otherwise would. People who would not save appreciably more for retirement than is assured to the destitute may rationally save nothing for retirement and count on charity or welfare. Social security reduces the scope of such behavior by compelling people to reduce current consumption in return for the assurance of future income. This gain from social security offsets and may override any losses attributed by standard economic analysis to restrictions that deter people from pursuing their own rational self-interest.[13]

In short, factors such as the unpredictability of unemployment, the imperfect rationality of many people regarding remote or improbable events, the fickleness of tastes, and the "moral hazard" created by assistance to the needy should be added to the standard economic model. It is not surprising that economists who apply this model without taking these complications into account conclude that social security is, at best, pointless and, at worst, harmful.

## CATEGORIES OF ECONOMIC MODELS

The effects of social security on economic behavior may be analyzed purely in theoretical terms, or one may look to statistics on actual behavior for evidence on the existence and magnitude of effects predicted from theoretical analysis. Theoretical analyses can be classified according to the planning horizon households are presumed to employ. In addition, one can make a distinction between pay-as-you-go and fully funded social security. A pay-as-you-go system means that in each year revenues approximate benefits paid. This condition implies that people who retire in the early years of the social security system receive benefits far larger in relation to taxes paid than will later cohorts. A system is always fully funded if at no point in the history of the system do retired cohorts receive benefits actuarially greater than those justified by the taxes they have paid.

The planning horizon of households may also be broken into two categories. "Life cycle" households plan the allocation of all resources available to them on the basis of their own wants, which may or may not include utility derived from bequests or gifts. "Multigenerational" households allocate the resources available to them *and their heirs* to maximize their own *and their heirs'* well-being.

These distinctions lead to four types of theoretical models for analyzing the effects of social security:

1. The fully funded, life cycle model
2. The fully funded, multigenerational model
3. The pay-as-you-go, life cycle model
4. The pay-as-you-go, multigenerational model[14]

In general, the first type of model leads to the conclusion that social security leaves economic behavior unaffected. As far as saving is concerned, households that wish to save for later consumption must reduce current consumption, build up assets that earn interest, and later deplete those assets. A funded social security system, defined as one in which people are promised benefits equal in actuarial value to the taxes they previously paid, mimics each step of private saving. The same kind of reasoning leads to the conclusion that social security will leave labor supply unaffected. Whatever social security can do, private decisions can undo, provided that households can borrow or lend freely and that the nature of the asset represented by social security benefits is essentially identical to assets available on the private market.

The third type of model leads to the conclusion that social security reduces saving significantly during the early years of the social security system and slightly thereafter. During the early years, beneficiaries receive benefits with an actuarial value far in excess of the taxes they have paid. Social security thereby enriches such households, providing what one economist has called a "lifetime wealth increment."[15] Although some part of this wealth increment may be transferred to others through gift or bequest, it normally results in increased consumption of both ordinary goods and leisure. More leisure means less hours of labor supplied, an effect which may be accentuated if the person receiving the increment must retire earlier than he or she otherwise intended in order to receive benefits. To the extent that people retire earlier than they otherwise would have done, however, they may be encouraged to save for the lengthened nonearning period.[16] Thus, models of this type lead to predictions that social security will cause people to reduce saving *or* labor supply *or* both.

The second and fourth models, those with multigenerational planning horizons, lead to predictions that social security normally leaves economic behavior unaffected. In the case of funded social security, the reasoning is identical to that for life-cycle planners. Assets held through a government program simply replace assets held by each household. In the case of pay-as-you-go social security, the reasoning differs. Beneficiaries in the early years of the social security system receive a wealth increment. But they understand that this benefit can come only at the expense of future generations, since total wealth available over time is not changed in any obvious way. Accordingly, the current generation increases the size of gifts and bequests to future generations to restore the distribution of income across generations that would have existed in the absence of social security. The current generation restores the intertemporal distribution of consumption. Total current consumption and current saving remain unaffected. Furthermore, because social security leaves long-run consumption and production possibilities unchanged, it does not reduce labor supply. In effect, the current generation chooses not to spend its increment in the form of increased leisure because of its concern for subsequent generations.

All of the analyses of the effects of social security presume that redistribution of income within cohorts has no material effect on saving or labor supply. To be sure, some families gain and others lose, but unless differences in consumption propensities or labor supply elasticities are substantial and are strongly correlated with redistribution, the effects of redistribution are of second order and may be disregarded.[17]

In summary, much of the economic theory being applied to social security in the mid–1980s suggests that social security does not produce many economic benefits. This conclusion derives from specific assumptions regarding the rationality of household behavior and the efficiency of markets. Following from these assumptions, the models imply that social security is likely to affect saving or labor supply if and only if individuals have planning horizons that do not look beyond their own lives and if early beneficiaries receive benefits greater in actuarial value than the taxes they have paid. These conditions correspond to a pay-as-you-go, life cycle model. The fact that this model closely approximates the behavior of many households has led economists who use life cycle models to assert that social security probably reduces both savings and labor supply.

## EMPIRICAL ESTIMATES

Attempts to measure the effects of social security on saving began in earnest following analysis by Feldstein in 1974 purporting to show that social security had reduced household saving by half. In subsequent years this conclusion was undermined by attacks on both the underlying theory and the econometric method. The coup de grace came in the form of a discovery that the conclusion was an artifact of a programming error, a series of arbitrary assumptions about how the present value of future social security benefits should be measured, and of the period over which data should be used for statistical estimation.[18] Correction of the programming error, *or* measurement of the present value of social security in any number of plausible alternative ways, *or* dropping data from one or two years led to estimates either that social security had no effect on saving or that social security had actually increased saving. These studies by Feldstein and by Leimer and Lesnoy form a minuscule fraction of the number of economic studies intended to measure the effect of social security on saving. On balance, the evidence is inconsistent, contradictory, and largely self-cancelling.[19]

Casual empiricism suggests that social security strongly reduces labor supply. The labor force participation rates of workers 65 or older have declined almost without interruption since World War II as the number of social security beneficiaries and benefits per retiree have increased. It would be easy, but an oversimplification, to attribute to social security this decline in labor force participation by older workers. Over the same period, other changes conducive to retirement have occurred. Eligibility for private pensions has increased, and pension amounts have risen. Increased wealth has repeatedly been shown to be a correlate of retirement, and workers have become wealthier through appreciation in the value of owned housing and the accumulation of other assets. Taking all measurable factors into account, most studies have concluded that the existence of social security encourages retirement, but some studies have concluded that it may increase labor supply. On such practical questions as whether change in the age at which benefits are payable would influence the timing of retirement there is a clear affirmative consensus. But the estimated effects of such changes on labor supply are surprisingly small.[20]

In general, social security may affect how much people save or work, but empirical analyses suggest that plausible variations in the program would produce small effects, if any. If policymakers conclude that saving or labor supply by older age cohorts should be increased, empirical research by economists on the effects of social security on such behavior suggests that the policymakers had better use other instruments if they want large effects.

## ECONOMICS, DEMOGRAPHY, AND THE FUTURE OF SOCIAL SECURITY

Two major demographic changes have caused renewed concern about the future of social security: the decline in the fertility rate between about 1965 and 1975, and the decline in mortality rates of the elderly beginning about 1970 and continuing to this day. Each raises the future cost of social security by increasing the ratio of beneficiaries to workers.

Official projections, such as the 1985 figures based on the intermediate or "IIb" assumptions, show the cost of currently legislated cash benefits falling from 11.3 percent of taxable payroll in 1985 to 10.2 percent of taxable payroll in 2004. The decline occurs because the relatively small cohorts born during the depression years reach retirement age between 1990 and 2004. Costs rise quickly as the baby boom generation reaches retirement age, and the smaller cohorts born after 1965 must shoulder the burden of the baby boomers' retirement benefits. By 2035, costs are projected to reach 15.9 percent of payroll, and they continue to exceed 15.5 percent of payroll until 2060 when the projections end.

If retirement benefits are currently financed by payroll taxes, active workers must pay increased taxes when retirement costs grow. The projected cost increases in social security raise questions about the likelihood of continued political support for the program and the manner in which increasing retirement costs should be spread among active workers. Economists can be expected to speak to each of these issues, although their discipline allows them to speak more authoritatively on the latter than on the former.

Economists have concluded that the historic income gap between the aged and the nonaged has narrowed and may have vanished.[21] Social security explains a large part of the improvement in the economic status of the aged. What do these facts suggest? First, social security cannot be scaled back without reducing the relative economic status of the aged. Second, increases in payroll taxes on the nonaged today may be inequitable because such taxes would place them at a relative disadvantage in comparison with current retirees.

The possibility that active workers might become resentful of the tax burdens they must shoulder to pay for retirement benefits, either today or in the next century, has led some observers to express the fear that a "generational war" might start in which social security would lose some of its political support. This emotive phrase is highly evocative but obscures clear thinking about both the costs of social security and the costs of retirement. If current payroll taxes are set approximately equal to current social security benefits, current payroll taxes (or some equal source of revenue) cannot be cut unless current benefits are cut. People who favor tax cuts must also favor cuts in current benefits, at least as social security is currently constituted. Yet few of those who acknowledge support for curtailing benefits favor reducing benefits for current retirees, presumably on the ground that retirees are poorly positioned to adjust to reductions in benefits.

The question of coping with future increases in retirement costs goes back to the 1930s debate over social security financing. Should current workers pay higher taxes than current benefits require so that a reserve can be built up? Such extra taxes increase the tax burden on the baby boom generation so that the increase in taxes on subsequent cohorts when the baby boomers retire will not be as large as it otherwise would be.

Discussions of the impact on future workers of increases in the cost of social security often focus on the hole instead of the doughnut. They pay more attention to how much the decline in the ratio of workers to retirees increases payroll taxes than to the impact on income after taxes. In 1985, the current cost of social security was estimated at about 11.1 percent of payroll, after accounting for the revenues derived from taxing benefits as specified in the 1983 amendments. This estimate implies a current cost payroll tax rate of 5.55 percent on the employer and 5.55 percent on the employee. On the assumption that the employer simply shifts his costs back on the employee, the worker's gross earnings in the absence of social security would have been 105.55 percent of his actual or nominal earnings. (This amounts to his present earnings, before social security gets deducted, plus the employer's share of social security which we are assuming the worker also pays.) In a similar manner, his earnings after payroll taxes would be 94.45 percent of his nominal earnings. (This amounts to the situation as it exists today, with the employee's share of social security being deducted from his check.) Now assume that the combined payroll tax increases to 15.2 percent (the projected peak current cost, net of income tax proceeds, under the intermediate assumptions). Gross earnings remain 105.55, and the employers' share continues to be shifted on the employee. The worker's nominal earnings fall to 98.1 percent of the previous nominal earnings level, the level at which the addition of the employer's share of the payroll tax (7.6 percent of the new nominal earnings level) produces gross earnings of 105.55. The employee also pays 7.6 percent of nominal earnings for social security. Deducting the worker's share from 98.1 produces earnings after payroll taxes of 90.6 percent of the prior nominal earnings level. Thus, under current-cost financing, as a result of the payroll tax increase, real income from earnings subject to social security taxation would fall from 94.5 percent to 90.6 percent of the previous nominal earnings level, a decline of 4.0 percent.

In addition, current law has scheduled a benefit reduction early in the next century in the form of an increase of two years in the age at which full benefits will be paid. A worker retiring today at age 63 receives a benefit equal to 86.67 percent of his full benefit. In 2035, a 63-year-old retiree will receive 75 percent of his full benefit. The increase in the retirement age reduces this social security benefit by 13.5 percent. If social security represents one-third of this retiree's income, the increase in the retirement age reduces the total income of the beneficiary by 4.5 percent. Since age 63 is close to the median age of retirement under social security and social security benefits equal at least one-third of the income of the aged, the retirement age change seems to have the effect of dividing the cost produced by demographic shifts about equally between future workers and future beneficiaries. (Or, more accurately, between the future workers' working years and retirement years, since future workers are also future beneficiaries.)

While the demographic shift increases the ratio of the elderly to the working-age population, it also reduces the ratio of children to the working-age population. Several economists have analyzed the impact of both changes on the total dependency burden to be shouldered by the working-age population, but none has yet analyzed satisfactorily all of the offsetting effects.[22]

To understand the net effect of demographic changes on social dependency costs, a number of facts must be considered simultaneously. Public expenditures per child are much lower than are expenditures per aged person. Thus, an increase in the ratio of the old to the young tends to boost public expenditures per dependent person. On the other hand, private sector expenditures per young dependent exceed private sector expenditures per aged dependent. Furthermore, expenditures on the young normally embody a higher investment component than do expenditures on the aged, suggesting that one should also consider the longer run effect on growth in per capita income of the decline in family size.

Only recently have economists analyzed what may be the most important effect of reduced birth rates on the per capita incomes of the baby bust generation. As the labor force shrinks, the capital stock per worker tends to rise. Since worker productivity rises with the per capita capital stock and wages rise with worker productivity, declining birth rates tend to increase before-tax wages. Two economists have modeled the effect of some of these influences on a stylized economy that provides social security with pay-as-you-go financing. When they simulated the effects of a decline in population growth from 2 percent a year to zero, they found a slight increase in per capita consumption.[23]

Recently, economists have also focused on the economics of household behavior and on intrafamily transfers. This work may lead to improved estimates of the net effect of the demographic shifts. For the moment, however, we have only a number of disparate straws in the wind with which to grasp this issue.

Congress does not wait for the results of economic analyses before it acts. In 1977, Congress accelerated future payroll tax increases enough to produce large projected surpluses. Changes adopted in 1983 made the expected reserves even larger. Under current projections, payroll taxes will exceed current cash benefits programs beginning in 1987. The surpluses will continue until about 2020. Thereafter, scheduled payroll tax rates fall below projected benefits.

This tax schedule will lead to the accumulation and subsequent decline of a trust fund balance projected to reach just under five years of expenditures in 2015. The balance in the fund will then equal about 25 percent of the country's gross national product. Thereafter, the retirement of the baby boom generation will increase annual expenditures, and the payroll tax will remain at the level first instituted in 1990. As a result, the trust fund, according to projections, will decline steadily until it is exhausted in 2049.

The current financing schedule has transformed what might have been a theoretical debate among academics about trust fund accumulation into a very practical debate about public policy. This debate allows economists to address simultaneously macroeconomic issues of tax and budget policy. In their initial response to Feldstein's 1976 proposal, many economists argued that increased government saving might be more apt to reduce aggregate investment through its immediate effect on GNP (lowering its rate of growth) than to increase investment through its longer run effect on the interest rate (lowering it and hence stimulating investment). They also argued that the relatively regressive incidence of the payroll tax made it a less desirable vehicle for increasing government saving than increases in the personal income tax. Presumably, these arguments are equally valid today. Another issue has arisen because of large and persistent deficits in federal non–social security activities. In the face of such deficits, social security surpluses may only prevent federal government activities from *reducing* national saving as much as they otherwise would do.

Our society can prepay some of the retirement costs of the baby boom generation but only if excess payroll tax revenues are translated into increased national saving. If excess payroll tax revenues merely replace other revenues, we merely will have financed some general fund expenditures through the payroll tax, and the accumulated balance in the trust fund will represent simply paper claims on future general fund resources. The drawing down of the trust fund balance will merely substitute future general fund expenditures for expenditures that would otherwise have been covered by payroll taxes.

In the past, many economists have doubted the beneficial effect of enhanced government savings on growth.[24] The current massive budget deficits have revived interest in this issue, however, and additional analyses of the effects of budget deficits may yield valuable insights about the effect of advance funding social security. Preliminary work suggests, for example, that if the social security accumulation is a net addition to national saving, then, after the year 2013, net labor income will be higher than it would have been in the absence of the trust fund accumulation.

## CONCLUSION

The interest of economists in social security is likely to grow as the number of retirees grows and benefits increase. Normative conclusions about whether social security increases or decreases welfare should be taken only as seriously as the models on which they are based. Predictions about the macroeconomic effects of alternative policies deserve greater credence, despite the spotty forecasting record of economists, because economic models underscore certain unavoidable trade-offs. Furthermore, they highlight certain complex interactions and provide a framework for analyzing them. Noneconomists should keep in mind, however, if they even need the reminder, that normative conclusions of complex models are sometimes obfuscated transformations of odd underlying assumptions. Perhaps economists, too, should keep this fact in mind.

## NOTES

1. Henry J. Aaron, *Economic Effects of Social Security* (Washington, D.C.: Brookings Institution, 1982); and Lawrence H. Thompson, "The Social Security Reform Debate," *Journal of Economic Literature* 21 (December 1983), pp. 1425–67 contain a more thorough review of the literature.

2. Paul H. Douglas, *Social Security in the U.S.: An Analysis and Appraisal of the Federal Social Security Act* (Westport, Conn.: Greenwood Press, 1972). This is a reprint of the 1936 edition cited in chapter 2. J. Douglas Brown, "Philosophical Basis of the National Old Age Insurance Program," in Dan McGill, ed., *Social Security and Private Pension Plans: Competitive or Complementary?* (Homewood, Ill.: Richard D. Irwin, 1977), pp. 1–13; Brown, *An American Philosophy of Social Security: Evaluation and Issues* (Princeton, N.J.: Princeton University Press, 1972); William Haber and Wilbur Cohen, eds., *Readings in Social Security* (New York: Prentice Hall, 1948).

3. Robert Myers and W. Andrew Achenbaum return to this point in later chapters of this volume. See Robert J. Myers, "Actual Cost of the Social Security System Over the Years Compared with 1935 Estimates," *Social Security Bulletin* 45 (March 1982), pp. 13–15.

4. Seymour E. Harris, *Economics of Social Security: The Relation of the American Program to Consumption, Savings, Output, and Finance* (Westport, Conn.: Greenwood Press, 1970), reprint of 1941 edition.

5. Martin S. Feldstein, "The Social Security Fund and National Capital Accumulation," in *Funding Pensions: Issues and Implications for Financial Markets, Proceedings of A Conference* (Boston: Federal Reserve Bank of Boston, 1976), pp. 32–64.

6. Alicia H. Munnell, *The Future of Social Security* (Washington, D.C.: Brookings Institution, 1977); Joseph A. Pechman, "The Social Security System: An Overview" in Michael J. Boskin, ed., *The Crisis in Social Security: Problems and Prospects* (San Francisco: Institute for Contemporary Studies, 1977), pp. 31–39; Selig D. Lesnoy and John C. Hambor, "Social Security, Saving, and Capital Formation," *Social Security Bulletin* 38 (July 1975), pp. 3–15.

7. Paul Samuelson, "An Exact Consumption-Loan Model With or Without the Social Contrivance of Money," *Journal of Political Economy* 66 (December 1958), pp. 467–82.

8. Peter Diamond, "A Framework for Social Security Analysis," *Journal of Public Economics* 8 (December 1977), pp. 275–98.

9. Alan S. Blinder, *Private Pensions and Public Pensions: Theory and Fact* (Ann Arbor: University of Michigan, 1981).

10. Daniel Kahnneman and Amos Tversky, "Judgment Under Uncertainty," in Peter Diamond and Michael Rothschild, ed., *Uncertainty in Economics* (New York: Academic Press, 1978).

11. Joseph Stiglitz, "Information and Economic Analysis: A Perspective," *Supplement to the Economic Journal* 95 (1984), pp. 21–41.

12. Thomas Schelling, *Choice and Consequence: Perspectives of an Errant Economist* (Cambridge, Mass.: Harvard University Press, 1984).

13. Martin Feldstein, "Should Social Security Be Means Tested?" National Bureau of Economic Research Working Paper no. 1775, December 1985.

14. Hirofumi Shibata, "Financing and the Politics of Financing Social Security Programs: An Analysis and Proposals for Reform," in *Public Finance and Social Policy: Proceedings of the 39 Congress of the International Institute of Public Finance* (Budapest, 1983), pp. 291–302.

15. Laurence Kotlikoff, "Testing the Theory of Social Security and Life-Cycle Accumulation," *American Economic Review* 69 (June 1979), pp. 396–411.

16. Martin Feldstein, "Social Security, Induced Retirement, and Aggregate Capital Accumulation," *Journal of Political Economy* 82 (September–October 1974), pp. 905–26.

17. Alan S. Blinder, "Distribution Effects and the Aggregate Consumption Function," *Journal of Political Economy* 83 (June 1975), pp. 447–75.

18. Dean Leimer and Selig Lesnoy, "Social Security and Private Saving: New Time Series Evidence With Alternative Specifications," *Journal of Political Economy* 90 (June 1982), pp. 606–42.

19. Henry J. Aaron, *Economic Effects of Social Security* (Washington, D.C.: Brookings Institution, 1982).

20. Gary Burtless and Robert A. Moffitt, "The Effect of Social Security Benefits on the Labor Supply of the Aged," in Henry J. Aaron and Gary Burtless, eds., *Retirement and Economic Behavior* (Washington, D.C.: Brookings Institution, 1984), pp. 135–74.

21. For a more complete discussion, see Henry J. Aaron, *Economic Effects of Social Security*.

22. Yung-Ping Chen and Kwang-wen Chu, "Total Dependency Burden and Social Security Solvency," *Proceedings of the Industrial Relations Research Association* (Industrial Relations Research Association, 1976); Robert L. Clark and Joseph J. Spengler, "Changing Demography and Dependency Costs: The Implications of Future Dependency Ratios and their Composition," in Barbara Rienman Herzog, ed., *Aging and Income: Programs and Prospects for the Elderly* (New York: Human Science Press, 1978), pp. 55–89.

23. Alan J. Auerbach and Laurence J. Kotlikoff, "Social Security and the Demographic Transition,"in Aaron and Burtless, eds., *Retirement and Economic Behavior*, pp. 255–76.

24. See, for example, Robert Eisner, "Government Policy, Saving and Investment," *Journal of Economic Education* 14 (Spring 1983), pp. 38–49.

# 5

# The Plight of the Social
# Security Administration

## MARTHA DERTHICK

Big government has produced big bureaucracies, about whose functioning we know very little apart from what we read in the newspapers.[1] And what we read there is not reassuring.

Within the past few years, newspapers have carried accounts of the Internal Revenue Service's struggle against record backlogs of unprocessed returns, hundreds of millions of dollars of erroneous or delayed refunds, incorrect dunning notices, unjustified threats to seize property, unanswered inquiries, and willful destruction of documents by employees seeking to meet production quotas.[2]

The misfortunes of the IRS recall numerous adverse stories about the Social Security Administration (SSA), the most extended and informative of which appeared in the *Washington Post* in 1977. In a three-part series, reporter Haynes Johnson portrayed the SSA—once the "brightest ornament in the . . . federal establishment"—as an example of "government gone awry."[3] Journalistic accounts of the SSA are reinforced by a variety of personal and official testimony that, given its origins, is entitled to some credence. A report to the National Commission on Social Security in 1980 by Jack S. Futterman, retired assistant commissioner of SSA for administration, described the agency as an "ailing mechanism" afflicted by low morale, poor staff work, unacceptably high levels of internal tension, and a declining ability to perform even routine tasks.[4] One might suppose that Futterman, a veteran of the agency's golden era, had succumbed to nostalgia, if his views were not shared by the relative newcomers who have presided over the agency recently. Stanford G. Ross, who was social security commissioner early in the Carter administration but had no prior connection with the agency, remarked in a recent speech on "substantial deficiencies in the facilities and functioning of the Social Security Administration." He called the information processing and computer systems "antiquated" and spoke of "substantial errors in the determination and delivery of benefits."[5] Innumerable findings of congressional committees, evaluations of the General Accounting Office (GAO), and recent reports by consultants and study panels say the same thing. Such comment has become the standard fare of the official and semiofficial source material on administration by the SSA.[6]

What follows is an effort to outline an inquiry into the causes of the SSA's poor performance. It suggests the logic by which such an inquiry might be pursued. A first step is to array explanations commonly offered.

## POSSIBLE CAUSES OF TROUBLE

Critiques of the SSA offer numerous indications that internal changes may be at the root of its difficulties. There are suggestions that the quality of its work force has declined. Consider, for example, the plaintive, carefully chosen words of Commissioner James B. Cardwell, reported in the *Washington Post* series of 1977:

> The concentration of so much of the agency's work in urban areas—and I've got to be careful how I say this because it could seem offensive to a lot of people—but it's highly probable that these urban areas no longer produce through their educational systems workers who are really qualified to do the work required. Yet they're the only workers you have. And those workers have now been mixed in with the original workers. Today they're probably dominant. They just behave differently about their work.[7]

The SSA has become heavily unionized, and this may have created unsolved problems for its supervisory staff. The words are again Cardwell's:

The government doesn't know anything about government-management relations. It's made one mistake after another. Today a supervisor of 100 people doing repetitive work should know something about management-labor relations. He should know something about how to motivate people, why people behave as they do. . . . It's very complex. . . . He isn't up to his job. And he isn't up to his job because the people you can hire for those salaries haven't been prepared for those jobs.[8]

Futterman's report focuses on the adverse effects of reorganizations on the SSA. Three occurred in the five years between 1974 and 1979. In his opinion, this drastic medicine, far from curing SSA's problems, exacerbated them. The objectives of the SSA's statutory programs lost their sharp focus when a functionally organized structure replaced a program-oriented one. To cite only a few of the unhappy consequences perceived by Futterman, managers lost control of staff support they needed to help them carry out their responsibilities efficiently, and centralized logistical and management support services deteriorated.

Failure to modernize computer technology is very often advanced as the crucial explanation of the deficiencies in the SSA's performance. The House Committee on Government Operations, for example, has issued scathing reports on this subject, such as this one in 1982:

The computer systems at SSA have been in steady deterioration for over a decade. Repeated attempts to correct the problems have failed. As a result, the current systems are on the brink of disaster. . . .

. . . SSA officials have mismanaged the critical operations of the agency over a period of decades. These officials have not acquired and used the advanced information technology that is critical to their operations . . . despite repeated warnings from GAO, Congress, and other audit agencies.[9]

Such internal factors, however, by no means exhaust the diagnoses of the SSA's troubles that can be gleaned from official and semiofficial sources. Factors external to the organization are also often cited, prominently including unstable policies, complex programs, poor support from government-wide staff agencies, and an imperfectly cooperative clientele.

"Frequent legislative changes have complicated program admin-istration," says a statement on the SSA's performance submitted to Congress in 1983 by the GAO, which is not often very sym-pathetic to the federal agencies that it scrutinizes. The report goes on to point out that the SSA is responsible for administering over 21 general types of benefits, whereas when social security began the program paid only retirement benefits (and a very small number of lump-sum death benefits, one might add, without detracting from the GAO's point). The GAO counted 92 changes in the monthly benefit calculation and 26 changes in the earnings test since the beginning of the program. From 1977 to 1982, over 6,200 bills were introduced in Congress pertaining to social security, and while only 66 of these passed, those that did contained 300 pro-visions that directly affected the SSA's administration of its various benefit programs.[10]

Benefit computations illustrate the extraordinary complexity of today's program. At one time, a retiree's basic benefit involved a simple computation applied to a worker's average monthly wage. Dependents and survivors were given a percentage of the basic benefit. Persons of ordinary competence might calculate their ben-efits themselves. However, the simplicity has given way to an ex-tremely complex series of computation methods and interacting conditions that make benefit computations out of the question for an ordinary person and very prone to error even when done by specialists. Congress has created provisions requiring new com-putation methods, but old ones typically are retained in law to give the beneficiary the benefit of whatever method provides the higher payment. Thus, even the simplest claims situation, Com-missioner Ross explained to Congress in 1979, required a minimum of three computations. For, say, a male wage earner retiring at 65, the SSA had to compute his potential benefits using all his earnings since 1937, and again using all earnings since 1950, and again using an index of earnings since 1950. To show the compli-cations, Ross then described a widow's case. First, if she had earned social security coverage in her own right, the agency had to make the three basic calculations done for any covered worker. It also had to make similar computations on her deceased hus-band's account and then pay her her own benefit plus the difference if the widow's benefit was higher. Ross proceeds as follows:

If she is under age 65 we must consider reduction of her benefit amount on both accounts at different reduction rates. If there are applicable annual benefit rate increases, we must also determine the number of months before age 65 she will actually receive benefits in order to determine the reduction rate that applies just to the benefit increase. Since she can also be a widow more than once, other computations may be necessary for any other such accounts.

Is she disabled? If so, a different reduction rate for benefits payable at a lower rate may be in order. Are delayed retirement credits in order? The widow's rate can be 100 percent of the deceased worker's rate including his delayed retirement credits but cannot exceed what he would have gotten had he lived. Had he drawn reduced benefits, for instance, her benefits would have to be reduced as well.[11]

Complexity, of course, is by no means confined to the benefit calculation but extends to the relationships among different income support programs and different governments within the federal system. Even the retirement and survivors program, which is administered solely by the SSA, is affected by differences in state laws, because the definitions of child-parent relationships in state law affect decisions about who is entitled to children's insurance benefits. In the disability insurance program and in the Supplemental Security Income (SSI) program, states make initial determinations of disability. The SSI program allows states to supplement the basic federally determined benefit and to choose whether this supplement should be administered by them or by the SSA. In both of these programs, therefore, the SSA is directly dependent on the states' cooperation.

From the heads of SSA field offices that serve the public come views that the agency's performance suffers because of lack of support from within the government. One told the *Post*'s Haynes Johnson in 1977:

If you were to ask me what are the largest barriers you have to overcome in order to do an efficient job, you know what my answer would be? The Civil Service Commission and the General Services Administration. These agencies . . . they do not serve us. They're there but they're there to block us. It's like they're in business for themselves. And their sole preoccupation is to keep themselves in power without rendering service.

Then, Johnson's account adds, "you will be told one horror story after another about problems in hiring clerical workers or getting office equipment or leasing new space."[12] If these quotations seem to suggest scapegoating or paranoia on the part of minor officials, it should be added that a highly critical view of the government's staff agencies is not confined to the lower management of the SSA. According to a recent study by the National Academy of Public Administration (NAPA), inefficient support and excessively detailed supervision from the central staff agencies hamper managers in many line agencies, managers who require much more autonomy if they are to perform well.[13] At the request of the Congressional Panel on Social Security Organization, NAPA extended its analysis specifically to the SSA, and found, for example, that Office of Personnel Management rules made it hard to recruit successfully among college graduates, the SSA's traditional source of new claims and service representatives. As a result, the quality of the agency's entry-level workforce was believed to be declining, thereby weakening the pool of personnel to fill supervisory and management positions.[14]

Complaints about other government agencies predominate over complaints about the public, but the official literature by and about the SSA contains, if not exactly complaints, numerous reminders that the accuracy of its administrative actions depends heavily on public cooperation. Although SSA can independently monitor some changes in beneficiary status, it needs notification from the beneficiaries for others, which often is not forthcoming. Individuals do not have to be willfully uncooperative in order to be uncommunicative.

Finally, to this long list of factors troubling the agency from without may be added one that is neither strictly internal nor external but partakes of both dimensions—namely, acute instability of leadership. The commissionership has turned into a revolving door. Even when the office is not empty, it is likely to be occupied by someone formally in "acting" status. Eight persons have held it since 1973. At the very least, this turnover has adversely affected agency morale. It may also have contributed indirectly to the other problems already mentioned, if only by making impossible a sustained, purposeful response to any one of them.

## ROUTINE VS. EXTRAORDINARY TASKS

There are so many possible explanations of faulty performance by the SSA that one hardly knows how to begin weighing them and analyzing their relative importance. Perhaps the most promising place to start is with the performance itself. Just how bad is it, and what is the evidence that it is bad? Is it worse in some activities than others? One way to approach these questions, and, one hopes, to make them more manageable, is to distinguish what the SSA does routinely from its extraordinary tasks.

As for routine tasks, the bulk of the SSA's work consists of issuing social security cards (6.7 million new ones and 6.6 million duplicates or replacements in 1983); receiving and posting earnings reports for virtually everyone in the country who is employed (170 million reports for 117 million workers in 1983); responding to inquiries from the public (40 million in 1983, including more than 50,000 from congressional offices on behalf of constituents); processing applications for benefits (5.5 million in 1983); and making benefit payments (to 35,840,000 persons in 1982, of whom 31,804,100, or nearly 90 percent, qualified under retirement and survivors insurance).[15]

The massive routines do not fail to generate complaints and signs of stress. Applicants for social security numbers complain that they have to wait too long. In 1981, for example, they waited an average of thirty-five days, and, in three cases out of ten, their wait lasted from six to eight weeks.[16] Backlogs have plagued the posting of earnings. According to a report that Commissioner John Svahn gave to Congress in 1983, these backlogs were attributable mainly to problems arising out of a break in the routines (namely, a switch in 1978 from quarterly to annual reporting by employers) and to a shortage of computer capacity. Giving first priority to payment of monthly benefits, the agency has lacked the computer time to run the program for crediting earnings as often as the agency would have liked.

For the monthly benefit payments—the raison d'être of the operation—the checks have gone out on time, but their accuracy is difficult to verify. Data are scarce, and estimates of error cover a wide range. A report to Congress by the GAO in 1983 suggests that if cases are observed long enough and closely enough, errors can be detected in a sizable proportion of payments. GAO reviewers had selected a national sample of 208 cases involving persons who became 68 in October in 1982 and were receiving retirement benefits. They had received an average of about $21,000 each over an average of about 55 months. About 41 percent of the sample had at least one initial claim, postentitlement, or payment error caused by the SSA (as distinct from the beneficiary). About 18 percent had payment errors, varying from less than $1 to over $4,800. About 32 percent had errors in documentation or notices to beneficiaries. Some of these errors were minor, such as the failure of a district office to certify a copy of a claimant's birth certificate. Other, more serious errors could have presented major problems for the beneficiaries.

The SSA routinely reports error rates considerably below what the GAO found. The difference appears to lie in differences in the scope of case actions and time periods reviewed. Whereas the GAO review covered all claims actions, postentitlement transactions, and payments over a period averaging more than four years, SSA's routine processing statistics are based on reviews of samples of individual claims, postentitlement transactions, and/or payments within periods of six months.[17]

Although not reassuring, such findings remain inconclusive. Perhaps the most disturbing feature of this information is its very thinness. The lack of reliable performance data that extend over time and are endorsed by both the agency and its official reviewers makes it impossible for an outsider who relies on public sources to pass judgment. By contrast, when one surveys the exceptional events in the SSA's recent history, the data become clearer and much more dramatic. Two such events patently warrant attention—the institution of the SSI program in the mid–1970s and the review of the eligibility of disability recipients begun in 1981.

## THE INSTITUTION OF SSI

Late in 1972, Congress completed action on P.L. 92–603, a set of amendments to the Social Security Act that federalized means-tested income support for the aged, blind, and disabled. That is, grants-in-aid to the states that dated from the early decades of federal welfare programs were abolished in favor of direct assumption of federal responsibility. Administration that had formerly been divided among the fifty state and several territorial governments now was concentrated in the SSA. A residual product of the Nixon administration's failed attempt to enact comprehensive welfare reform, the creation of SSI marked an unusual event in American public administration. On the whole, Congress has preferred to rely on influencing the states through grant-in-aid conditions or regulations rather than on superseding state administration. To the extent that the hearings preceding this change discuss administration at all, they convey great confidence that federal administration would inevitably be much more efficient than what it was to replace.

Congress gave the SSA fourteen months to make the transition; the new programs went into effect at the beginning of 1974. They had not been under way very long before it became clear that the confidence displayed in the hearings had been excessive. The administrative beginnings of SSI were beset by a host of problems.

Late in November 1975, House overseers of SSI reported "unacceptable delays," "errors in payments," and a failure to "enroll up to 2 million eligible individuals." According to Charles Vanik, the chairman of the Subcommittee on Oversight of the House Ways and Means Committee, only half of the computer support systems were ready, efforts to find eligible recipients had not been started, the estimates of the number of people the SSA would be able to serve with available personnel were badly mistaken, and the speed with which the SSA could process cases had been overstated. Furthermore, Vanik noted that "no checks were made on the quality of case data transferred from the States to the SSI rolls, with the result that error rate was very high and has forced SSA to 'redetermine' the cases twice."[18]

A report by the staff of the Senate Finance Committee in 1977 declined to join in the House's criticism of the SSA's "outreach" efforts, but otherwise presented a similar picture, while adding to the indictment that the SSA had flouted Congress's intent. It said that in the early months of the program there had been a "near total administrative breakdown" as a result of "insufficient and inaccurate planning and administrative resources." The report went on to say that:

The administering agency has repeatedly ignored the law in making
policy decisions which run directly contrary to the statute and its
legislative history; these policy decisions have distorted the nature
of the program and have significantly increased the difficulty of
administering it.[19]

## THE DISABILITY REVIEW

The saga of the disability review begins a mere five years later.
The Social Security Disability Amendments of 1980 (P.L. 96–265)
became law in the middle of that year. They responded to a widespread concern that the disability program was growing uncon-
trollably and benefiting persons who could in fact work. One
provision, little discussed yet widely endorsed at the time, required
that, beginning in January 1982, the Secretary of Health and Human Services review every three years the eligibility of all beneficiaries who had been found not to be permanently disabled.

In March 1981, the SSA began implementing the newly required
review, nine months before the law required it to. A major reason
for the decision to begin so quickly was the appearance (during
the transition from the Carter to the Reagan administration) of a
draft report by the GAO indicating that as many as one in five
workers on the disability rolls might be ineligible and that the
payment of benefits to ineligible persons might be costing as much
as $2 billion per year. The report urged the SSA to redirect all
available resources toward removing ineligible individuals from
the disability insurance rolls. Studies by the SSA itself had said
that a substantial proportion of recipients did not meet the legal
definition of disability.[20] There may also have been administrative
reasons for moving swiftly. If the SSA had started the new mandatory review in January 1982, the state agencies that make disability determinations would have had to process about 500,000
reviews in fiscal year 1982 in addition to their regular load; by
starting in March 1981, the additional burden could be spread over
a longer period. And, finally, the politics of budget-cutting very
likely had an effect. The Reagan administration was in the first
flush of its attack on federal spending. The disability rolls were a
ready-made target, at which David Stockman's Office of Management and Budget did not fail to take aim. Reagan's "Program for

Economic Recovery," announced in February 1981, promised that under the "new management team" disability benefits would no longer be "misdirected."[21]

Problems in disability insurance administration were not unrelated to those in SSI. The initiation of SSI, which was accompanied by fresh efforts at administrative "outreach," appears to have stimulated a large number of new applications for disability insurance. Applications reached a record high (over 1.3 million) in 1974, the year SSI began, and the number of new awards, at 592,000, reached an all-time high in 1975. At the same time, SSI so burdened the SSA that its capacity to make disability decisions or to review those made by the states was impaired. Even before SSI was instituted, signs of declining administrative capacity were manifest. Yielding to budget pressures, the SSA in 1972 had sharply reduced its reviews of the eligibility of disability cases—both the reviews done at the time of the initial determination by state agencies and those done later to confirm continuing eligibility. These administrative problems were some of the reasons, although certainly not the only ones, for believing as of 1980 that the program was out of control and benefiting persons of doubtful eligibility.[22]

Under the new statutory requirement for review, over a million disability cases were examined in fiscal years 1982 and 1983. The termination rate originally ran at close to 50 percent. It then hovered around 45 percent for more than a year, and it dropped below 40 percent in the last half of 1983. There are numerous opportunities for appeal of decisions denying disability benefits, and many of those who had their benefits terminated chose to use them. From February 1982 through September 1983, administrative law judges (ALJs) heard 152,000 appeals and reversed the decision to terminate in 92,000 of them (61 percent). At the end of September 1983, 173,000 appeals cases were pending before ALJs. Individuals were waiting from six to twelve months to get a hearing, at which an ALJ was likely to decide that they had been entitled to benefits all along. The federal courts likewise were inundated. For the three years from 1982 to 1984, about 62,000 new disability suits were filed. The pending caseload rose from about 27,000 at the end of 1982 to nearly 50,000 at the end of 1984. District and circuit courts repeatedly ruled against the SSA both in individual cases and in class actions that challenged guidelines and administrative practices, although the agency won an important victory in the Supreme Court in 1983 over the validity of its medical-vocational guidelines, used in evaluating claims for disability in which vocational factors must be considered.

Partly because the SSA was suffering frequent defeats in the courts, it also began to encounter resistance from the states, upon whose agencies it depended to conduct the review. Eighteen of them, including Massachusetts, New York, Virginia, Pennsylvania, Michigan, Illinois, Ohio, Maryland, and North Carolina, halted terminations in 1983–1984, refusing to carry out the SSA's directives any longer. Congress, in turmoil, responded by holding twenty-seven hearings between 1982 and 1984, thirteen of them outside of Washington, at which aggrieved victims of the review appeared, often with stories of manifest injustice and extraordinary hardship.[23]

In 1984, Congress passed a law designed to "restore order, uniformity, and consensus in the disability program," in the words of President Reagan's signing statement. It sought to define with some specificity the conditions under which disability benefits might be terminated.[24] Thus was brought to an end one of the most discreditable events in the recent history of American public administration.

## APPROACHES TO INTERPRETATION

There must be better ways to run a government, and trying to detect the sources of recent deficiencies in the SSA's performance is one approach to discerning them. Even if not typical, these two dramatic cases are a promising place to begin such an inquiry. Even the meager sketches I have given are sufficient to suggest that the answers will not be simple. Administrative performance cannot realistically be divorced from policymaking, which defines the administrative task. The SSA cannot be analyzed in isolation from its institutional context. And in the background, affecting everything, lie the sheer size of the present undertaking and reactions to that size.

It is important to grasp how drastically the scale of social insurance operations has changed in our own lifetimes. As recently as 1950, the SSA employed only 11,000 persons. By 1960 this number had grown to 25,000; by 1970, to 50,000; and by 1980, to 75,000. Managing an organization of 75,000 is a different order of undertaking than managing one of 11,000. The latter population makes up only a very big town; the former, a medium-sized city. The number of beneficiaries has multiplied much faster, rising from 3.5 million in 1950 to 35.6 million in 1980. As a share of the U.S. population, it rose from 2 to 16 percent. Benefit payments went from $783 million in 1950 to $117 billion in 1980, but again the proportions are probably more telling. As a share of U.S. Government outlays, social security rose from 2 percent in 1950 to 20 percent in 1980.

Apart from its other effects, such as compounding the challenge of organizational management, size itself elicits a response, the more so as the size of federal budget deficits also rises. Unprecedented efforts at control emanate from the Executive Office of the President, or the Office of the Secretary of Health and Human Services, or, occasionally, segments of the Congress. These efforts did not begin with the arrival of President Reagan. They go back to the Nixon administration, especially the second Nixon administration. They are not confined to Republican presidencies. The Democratic administration of Jimmy Carter looked for ways to contain social security spending and thereby touched off personal confrontations of furious intensity—the kind that occur within families or circles of friends when members betray one another.[25]

The new emphasis on control appears to have slowed down the SSA's implementation of SSI and speeded up its implementation of the disability review, to the detriment of each. In the former case, the agency had to address time-consuming justifications of its requests for more staff and facilities to essentially unsympathetic overseers in the second Nixon administration, who were less than enthusiastic about the "achievement" of welfare reform embodied finally in SSI. In the latter case, cues from a wide array of external sources, including Congress and Congress's agent, the GAO, had urgently and unmistakably told the SSA to get the disability rolls under control.

That the SSA faced these commands, cues, and constraints under new leaders—or, at intervals, with *no* leader—is also attributable in some measure to the new political context. The emphasis on control has led administrations to prefer commissioners from outside the agency. At the least, they have been less "professional" than those of the past, meaning less engaged in social security as a career. Beyond that, some have also been "political" in the sense of having been active in the service of a party or a particular presidential candidate. With the change in the nature of appointments to the commissionership has come a sharply accelerated turnover of the appointees. The turnover may not be greater than that typical of political appointees in the federal government, but it is much greater than was characteristic of the SSA's leadership in the past.

For an agency imbued with a sense of social mission and long accustomed to exceptional autonomy and stability of leadership, the new context of control has been deeply demoralizing and disorienting. And this condition is not relieved, but in all probability is made worse, by the fact that the policy cues emanating from the environment by no means consistently support constraint. The policy and institutional context, though obviously changed, is itself unstable and confused. On the whole, court decisions are very much at odds with the presidential-level effort to contain costs, which itself is only intermittent and contingent. Congress meanwhile shows no consistency at all, taking one side or the other— or both at the same time—in response to the stimulus of events and surges of vocal opinion.

These institutions produce so much criticism of administration that one can hardly charge them with being indifferent to it. Yet even the most superficial review of administrative events, such as is contained in this essay, leads one to ask how carefully Congress, the presidency, and the courts weigh the administrative consequences of their own acts and where administrative performance falls in the hierarchy of concerns on which policymaking and adjudication are premised.

What stands out from the SSI and disability review cases is a comprehensive failure—embracing, it would appear, the SSA itself and its overseers in every branch—to appreciate and attend to the administrative consequences of significant policy change. Any attempt to appraise the recent performance of the SSA must above all pursue the explanation for that failure. It must ask what questions about administration public officials ask of themselves and one another as they go about their work.

## NOTES

1. There are relatively few empirical and analytical studies of federal administrative agencies and no current, comprehensive studies of the two biggest agencies, the Social Security Administration and the Internal Revenue Service. Jerry L. Mashaw, *Bureaucratic Justice* (New Haven: Yale University Press, 1983), deals exclusively with SSA's management of disability claims. On other agencies, see Herbert Kaufman, *The Forest Ranger* (Baltimore: Johns Hopkins University Press, 1960); and James Q. Wilson, *The Investigators* (New York: Basic Books, 1976).

2. Kathy Sawyer, "The Mess at the IRS," *Washington Post National Weekly Edition*, November 11, 1985.

3. Haynes Johnson, "Days of Endless Struggle, Drowning in a Sea of Paper," *Washington Post*, March 27, 1977, pp. 1, A15; "Social Security: U.S. Umbilical Cord," *Washington Post*, March 28, 1977, pp. 1, A8–9; "Government Gone Awry," *Washington Post*, March 29, 1977, pp. 1, A6. See also the series by John Fialka in late August 1975 in the *Washington Star*, dealing specifically with the Social Security Administration's troubles in administering the Supplemental Security Income program.

4. Jack S. Futterman, "Report to the National Commission on Social Security," July 28, 1980, unpublished document, pp. 23–25.

5. Stanford G. Ross, "Public and Private Aspects of Social Policy: What Are the Appropriate Roles for Public and Private Sector Programs?" unpublished paper delivered at Brandeis University, November 1985, pp. 25–26.

6. Among many examples, see Subcommittee on Social Security, Committee on Finance, U.S. Senate, *Administrative Integrity of the Social Security Program* (Washington, D.C.: Government Printing Office, 1979); Congressional Panel on Social Security Organization, *A Plan to Establish an Independent Agency for Social Security (Senate Print 98–204)* (Washington, D.C.: Government Printing Office, 1984).

7. *Washington Post*, March 28, 1977.

8. Ibid. On federal unionization see Sar Levitan and Alexandra B. Noden, *Working for the Sovereign* (Baltimore: Johns Hopkins University Press, 1983).

9. House Committee on Government Operations, *Mismanagement of SSA's Computer Systems Threatens Social Security Programs (House Report 97–900)* (Washington, D.C.: Government Printing Office, 1982), p. 15.

10. "Statement of Joseph F. Delfico, Associate Director, Human Resources Division, General Acounting Office, before the Special Committee on Aging, U.S. Senate, on Social Security Administration's

Performance in Providing Public Service, November 16, 1983," unpublished manuscript, November 16, 1983, pp. 14–15.

11. Subcommittee on Social Security, Committee on Finance, *Administrative Integrity of the Social Security Program* (Washington, D.C.: Government Printing Office, 1979), pp. 27–28.

12. Johnson, "Days of Endless Struggle," *Washington Post*, November 27, 1977.

13. *Revitalizing Federal Management: Managers and Their Overburdened Systems*, A Panel Report of the National Academy of Public Administration, November 1983, privately distributed.

14. "The Social Security Administration: Management Reforms As a Part of Organizational Independence," May 1984, Appendix F to Congressional Panel on Social Security Organization, *A Plan to Establish an Independent Agency for Social Security (Senate Print 98–204)* (Washington, D.C.: Government Printing Office, 1984).

15. Most of these data are from *A Plan to Establish an Independent Agency for Social Security*, pp. 8–9, but I have also drawn on Office of Management, Budget and Personnel, Social Security Administration, *Executive Handbook of Selected Data (Social Security Administration Publication 24–085)*.

16. Committee on Ways and Means, Subcommittee on Social Security, *Administration of the Social Security Program, Serial 97–37* (Washington, D.C.: Government Printing Office, 1981), pp. 28–39.

17. United States General Accounting Office, "Statement of Joseph F. Delfico," November 16, 1983.

18. U.S. House of Representatives, Committee on Ways and Means, *Administration of the Supplemental Security Income Program*, vol. 1 (Washington, D.C.: Government Printing Office), p. 3.

19. U.S. Senate, Committee on Finance, *The Supplemental Security Income Program. Report of the Staff of the Committee on Finance* (Washington, D.C.: Government Printing Office, 1977), p. 3.

20. For a comprehensive review of these events see Katharine P. Collins and Anne Erfle, "Social Security Disability Benefits Reform Act of 1984: Legislative History and Summary of Provisions," *Social Security Bulletin* 48 (April 1985), pp. 5–32. I have relied heavily on this source. In addition, see Edward Berkowitz's forthcoming Twentieth Century Fund report on disability policy, to be published by Cambridge University Press in spring of 1987.

21. "America's New Beginning: A Program for Economic Recovery," February 18, 1981, cited in David Koitz to James M. Shannon, "Administration's Role in the Periodic Review of Disability Cases," June 22, 1983.

22. See the analysis in *Staff Data and Materials Related to the Social Security Disability Insurance Program*, Committee Print of the Committee on Finance, U.S. Senate, 97th Congress, 2d session, 1982, CP 97–16, pp. 17ff. This analysis also stressed rising benefit levels, which increased the attractiveness of the program.

23. Collins and Erfle, "Social Security Disability Benefits Reform Act of 1984"; David Koitz, "Social Security: Reexamining Eligibility for Disability Benefits," *Issue Brief 82078* (Washington, D.C.: Congressional Research Service, 1984).

24. Collins and Erfle, "Social Security Disability Benefits Reform Act of 1984," pp. 5–11.

25. Joseph Califano, *Governing America* (New York: Simon and Schuster, 1981), chap. 9.

# 6

# Social Security: A Source of Support for All Ages

## W. ANDREW ACHENBAUM

Social security—the nation's largest and most successful domestic program—has reached a critical juncture in its development.[1] Old-age, survivors, disability, and hospital insurance (OASDHI) no longer enjoys solid popular support. Senior citizens worry that their benefits will be cut. Many younger Americans fear that social security will not exist when they are retired. Social security, once viewed as an institution whose importance transcended petty politics, now is at the center of partisan debates over the federal deficit.

Social security's basic orientation has not changed much over time. The program's faithful loyalists have consistently maintained that it is an enduring source of support for all age groups. When times were good, the economy was booming, and public confidence in the government was high, few people expressed concern over the limits to extending the principle of social insurance in the United States. As long as the number of new contributors far exceeded the number of beneficiaries, legislators could liberalize existing provisions, expand coverage, and increase average benefits—and still point to huge surpluses in trust funds. Nurturing mutual responsibility through federal initiatives was a relatively inexpensive investment.

Such a felicitous set of circumstances could not last forever. The program's creators fully recognized that, as the system matured, adjustments would have to be made in social security's structure and financing. They could not have foreseen, however, that the transitional period would coincide with a decade of serious economic dislocation, political upheaval, and social unrest. The optimistic, expansionist philosophy that inspired planning after World War II changed to one of guarded hope that the best of the past could be preserved while addressing the considerable needs of the future. The crisis mentality of the last decade makes it difficult to persuade a skeptical electorate and conservative critics that implementing technical modifications will work unless the serious policy issues that have shadowed social security since its formative years are faced. Paradoxically, the boomerang effects of incremental policymaking (wherein legislative victories have sown the seeds for systemic confusions later on) no less than the mounting frustrations associated with ad hoc recalibrations (that quickly fail to live up to policymakers' and voters' expectations) demonstrate the importance of turning our attention to major issues—those nagging questions that have long surrounded the objectives and scale of social insurance in the United States.

The future of social security hangs in the balance. We are less confident than ever before about the risks we can expect the federal government to underwrite. To put the issue bluntly: How much social insurance can we really afford? The case for social security must be made for generations of Americans who never lived through a Great Depression and cannot remember a time when the federal government did not play a major role in their lives.

The 1983 social security amendments succeeded for the moment in defusing the financial crisis in social security. OASDI trust funds appear solvent for the next half-century. Actuaries do not expect a shortfall in the HI trust fund for at least a decade. Yet just because we have cleared up some financing woes does not mean that there are no longer key matters of social policy before us. The problems that may becloud social insurance are not just actuarial or fiscal in nature, even though that is how they are usually viewed. Economic concerns are assuredly relevant, but they do not constitute the crux of the matter.

If we choose not to confront some of the critical questions that have shadowed debates over social insurance since the progressive era, then I predict that the 1983 amendments will become yet another instance of tinkering with the system in ways that prolong the threat of a "legitimacy crisis." On the other hand, if we select the opportunity to use the 1983 amendments as the basis for reasserting and clarifying goals and objectives that policymakers should keep in mind as they face the future, we can reorient OASDHI as it comes of age in an aging society. For Congress provided vital precedents—and left the door open—to rework the program in light of the cumulative impact of past policy decisions and in the face of pertinent societal trends that have too often been ignored. We must construct a coherent policy framework out of the implicit preferences and conflicting signals crafted in the technical changes embodied in this crucial piece of legislation.[2]

## THE DEVELOPMENT OF SOCIAL SECURITY

From the start, policymakers intended social insurance to afford protection against specific hazards associated with successive stages of life. Franklin Delano Roosevelt and his advisors concentrated on the plight of the aged poor because, in the 1930s, old-age dependency was a major problem inadequately relieved by existing programs. The Great Depression had rent asunder the elderly's safety net. Firms stopped paying stipends to their superannuated workers. Private charities were overwhelmed by the increased demand for assistance. Local and state relief agencies imposed stringent eligibility criteria but, even then, could not help everyone in dire straits.[3]

Desperate, the elderly wrote to Washington pleading for help. Some older supplicants stressed that they could not feed, clothe, and shelter their adult children who were out of work. Middle-aged citizens sometimes wrote on behalf of their parents and the older generation:

> Well, whither [*sic*] my mother ever gets anything or not, I hope all the other old people that is intitled to it gets it soon, because there is nothing sadder than old people who have struggled hard all there lives to give there family a start in life, then to be forgotten, when they them self need it most.[4]

Policymakers sought to transcend the immediate economic crisis by providing a measure of security for all citizens. Through social insurance, the federal government committed itself to underwriting a system of income transfers that benefited every age group. The elderly would receive relief and future protection; their middle-aged kin would be free to devote their attention to their children. By coordinating the old-age insurance program with a system of old-age assistance, the federal government was adopting a plan that "amounts to having each generation pay for the support of the people then living who are old."[5] The principles underlying Titles I and II suggest a genuine—and imaginative—concern for addressing the vicissitudes of old age in the context of the family and the passage of generations.

In drafting the original legislation, a critical choice was made that greatly influenced the development of social security. The 1935 act established categorical programs that used "age" as a surrogate for identifying various social risks. But the elderly were not the only beneficiaries. Several titles dealt with the needs of citizens who were not old. Congress appropriated $4 million for the first year and at least $49 million annually thereafter under Titles III and IX for the new federal-state unemployment compensation program. Nearly $25 million was earmarked for aid to dependent children under Title IV; another $3 million was to be spent on relief to the blind—Title X. And just as Title II facilitated the current working population's ability to prevent hardships in the years ahead, so too the architects of social security took steps to promote the general welfare of future generations. Under Title V, Congress appropriated more than $9 million for crippled children, rural public services, and vocational rehabilitation; another $10 million was given to the Public Health Service for training new personnel and investigating diseases—Title VI.

The pivotal 1939 amendments altered both social security's pool of potential recipients and its financing of transgenerational protection. Probably the most significant change was that Congress established monthly benefits for the survivors and dependents of retired workers. By introducing a whole new set of eligibility criteria and payment schedules for elderly wives, aged widows, widows with children, dependent children, surviving children, and, under certain circumstances, the needy parents of workers who had died, policymakers underscored the importance of maintaining the family's integrity. "Safeguarding the family against economic hazards is one of the major purposes of modern social legislation," observed John McCormack in the House debate. "Old-age legislation, contributory and noncontributory, unemployment compensation, mothers' aid, and general relief by several States and then political subdivisions, aid to the blind and incapacitated, all have an important bearing on preserving the family life."[6] However, lawmakers did not devote as much attention to provisions affecting the unemployed, dependent children, and the blind as they did Titles I and II. Social security advocates increasingly became preoccupied with the societal risks associated with the latter stages of the life course.

Old-age dependency was not the most important hazard of modern life, but public officials were convinced that alleviating this risk would have a ripple effect throughout society, which would work to the advantage of all age groups. Providing more security in this area, they hoped, would not only bolster public morale, but also make citizens more security-conscious and thereby increase concern for protecting themselves and their children to the best of their ability.[7] Policymakers were willing to underwrite additional protection for older people because they believed that—in the long run—it would benefit an aging society.[8]

After World War II, OASI evolved in an incremental manner. Age 65 increasingly became perceived as the benchmark for the onset of old age. Over time, Congress instituted other age-based eligibility criteria. The inauguration of the disability program and efforts to liberalize Title II to adapt to the changing roles of women and men reinforced the significance of defining coverage against risks on the basis of age. This administratively straightforward procedure avoided the stigma of "welfare" associated with some means-testing formula. Indeed, Americans preferred that government officials reduce the risks of dependency but take no initiative jeopardizing a fair return—and ideally, a handsome profit—on investments of time and energy. "A high level of economic security is essential for maximum production," observed John Kenneth Galbraith in his seminal *Affluent Society*.[9]

The strategy of broadening social security coverage and benefits in a careful and deliberate manner proved successful for more than twenty-five years. Most commentators were convinced that the landmark 1972 amendments were yet another instance of the efficacy of the politics of incrementalism. Edwin L. Dale, who wrote on economic affairs for the *New York Times*, was persuaded that

> social security at the worst is not a bad deal and is safe, even for the young worker with 40 years of paycheck deductions ahead of him. It is not a bad deal, either, for the doctors and salesmen and other self-employed who tend to do the most squawking. Unless the world blows up or the country goes bankrupt, it is highly likely that current workers will get back from social security more than they paid in if they live only a few years past their retirement age, and a great deal more if they live a long life.[10]

This line of reasoning still makes sense, but the age-specific nature of current entitlements often distracts us from remaining faithful to one of the most appealing features of the program's original vision. Social security clearly is older Americans' most important source of economic support, but the old are not the only people who benefit from social insurance. Roughly a quarter of all Title II beneficiaries in 1940 were children; forty-five years later, one out of eight recipients was under the age of 18. Most workers (more precisely their dependents and survivors, in case of disability or premature death) are potential beneficiaries.[11] OASDHI's value to an average person through life needs to be emphasized in any campaign to reduce intergenerational tensions.

Thoughtful commentators and policymakers have always been concerned that the enactment and maturation of a governmental social insurance program might pit the genuine, immediate claims of the old against the legitimate, future interests of the young. In forecasting a nation of elders in the making earlier in the century, social scientists and journalists speculated that satisfying the financial needs of older Americans might disrupt national production, consumption, and inheritance patterns, and thereby threaten the stability of the country's economic and political institutions. "In no other country," observed a writer in 1933, "does the basis of age alone furnish so definite a line between a portion of the population recognized as economically efficient and socially attractive and that part of it which is neither useful nor particularly attractive."[12]

The potential for conflict between the needs of working people and the retired revived in the late 1970s. Analysts argued that policies adopted to meet the demands and problems of an ever-growing elderly population might be "busting the U.S. population." Many predicted that the situation would only get worse as the graying of America continued. More than 25 percent of the federal budget was already being allocated to underwrite the nation's old-age retirement and health-care delivery systems. As the number of Americans living past 75 soars, costs inevitably will skyrocket.[13]

Not surprisingly, public-opinion polls reveal that older people have more faith in the program than younger respondents. Men and women who think they will receive something doubt that social security will prove to be as good an investment for them as it was for their parents and grandparents.[14] In a marked switch from the overwhelming support that OASDHI had enjoyed in its formative years, Americans suddenly evinced considerable fears about social security's soundness. Media reports fanned concern. "Every time the press writes that social security has money problems," complained one congressman, "we get a ton of letters and phone calls from people who want to be reassured."[15]

Senior citizens increasingly were portrayed in stereotypical ways. Those who wanted to show how blissful the elderly were compared to the rest of the population interviewed healthy residents in Sun City. Those who viewed the aged as drains on productivity and economic growth took a hard-nosed look at "dependency" and looked askance at able-bodied couples enjoying their leisure time. Indeed, some argued that the current rules are rigged to give senior citizens far more than was originally intended. According to Philip Longman, age 26:

In enforcing their claims of generational privilege, the old undermine the younger generation's opportunity to enjoy the prosperity of its elders. . . . That portion of the nation's limited wealth squandered on its unneedy old must be subtracted in equal measure from what can be invested toward future economic growth. The magnitude of these entitlements thus compromises the young's very ability to finance them, a conundrum made far more unjust by yet another burden: The unpaid bills the old have left behind.[16]

The inevitability of intergenerational warfare can be exaggerated, of course. The range of assets, interests, and needs of the elderly population are too diverse to foster their mobilization as a monolithic, single-minded political force. There simply is no evidence yet that advocates of the aged's rights take a position on social security that is at odds with the views expressed by groups advancing the interests of children or young people. More important, the middle-aged children usually do not organize along age-specific coalitions. Their role in mediating among the interests of various age groups is paramount.[17] Nevertheless, if current Title II entitlements seem unduly generous, then support for social insurance becomes commensurately precarious. Proceeding on the belief that one age group benefits at the expense of another will hamper rational consideration of the nation's welfare priorities and resources en bloc.

Many neoliberals and neoconservative critics who are in the vanguard of the baby boom birth cohort are suggesting that it is now politically and economically feasible to reduce the relative importance of federal expenditures for old-age and survivors insurance. Such a tack is possible. But proposals to constrain the future growth of OASI merit serious consideration only if they were implemented while increasing pension coverage and average retirement benefits under other retirement resources in the private and public sectors. Whatever savings are ultimately realized in the area of income maintenance, moreover, should be earmarked to cover other social insurance expenditures, especially those related to the health care needs of very young and very old Americans. Considering these steps, in my opinion, requires us to transcend the artificial boundaries reified in categorical programs and to move beyond erroneous assumptions about OASDHI's purposes and operations.

We should begin by acknowledging that there never has been a genuine consensus in this country over what constitutes a credible and sound social security program. Americans surely count on receiving something if they become disabled or widowed or when they retire, but there is no empirical research for asserting that they plan their lives around current rules, much less that they truly understand how the program operates. Furthermore, precisely because the structure and dynamics of American life will continue to change in the future, policymakers are in a bind. They must act as if they can anticipate developments down the road, knowing full well that they cannot begin to divine the future. Future problems and opportunities surely will not be the same as those in the present, but public officials must act as if they will be. Hence, in presenting its views on the long-term financial status of the nation's social insurance program, the 1938 Advisory Council solemnly affirmed that "we should not commit future generations to a burden larger than we would want to bear ourselves."[18] Similarly, as President Reagan signed the 1983 amendments into law, he declared that "the changes in this legislation will allow social security to age as gracefully as all of us hope to do ourselves, without becoming an overwhelming burden on generations still to come."[19] To fail to pay obeisance to future generations is politically dangerous. To pretend that one knows what burdens future Americans have been spared is more than a little presumptuous.

To provide continuous protection over the life course does not necessitate arbitrary trade-offs between young and old. Rather than dwell on the competing interests of different cohorts, it would be wiser to develop programs that build on the fact that we live in a society in which the life cycle itself has become fluid. Becoming 65 no longer conjures up the image of obsolescence that once prevailed. Indeed, in an aging society—one in which two-thirds of all the changes in life expectancy have taken place since 1900— the future steps of the aged can most effectively be addressed by taking steps to enhance people's opportunities at earlier stages of their lives. Demographic trends are not the only factors at play here. During the past fifty years the labor force has become more heterogeneous. Differences between blue collar and white collar workers have become less obvious as variations in earnings potential and retirement income by gender, race, and education have grown more significant. Distinguishing between the public and private sectors of employment has become anachronistic. Current definitions of risk, which presume that normal hazards occur at predictable stages of life, cannot take account of such diversity. The goal of social insurance must be to provide economic security—a living wage—for working people who find themselves in very different circumstances at various stages of life.

Similarly in establishing rights under social insurance, we must bear in mind that social security properly deals with the setting of human life rather than presuming either that government knows best how individuals choose to live their lives, or that government does best when it encourages Americans to think of themselves as a crowd of individuals pursuing their dreams in a free market. In making successive changes in the Social Security Act, Congress has reserved the "right to alter, amend, or repeal any provision"— a right no Supreme Court ruling has ever challenged. Rather than bemoan this historical truth, we should take advantage of it. Recognizing that social security is not the only way to provide for the vicissitudes of life means that we simply cannot afford to discuss the program's goals and financing in a vacuum. Policymakers must take account of the role that other institutions—the family, the church, voluntary groups, private organizations—play in American contemporary life. These mediating institutions facilitate our individual or collective efforts to attain a measure of security from the risks of modern times. They afford the average American an extraordinary range of options and thereby promote individual choice.

## POLICY RECOMMENDATIONS

What the nation needs is better—and sometimes indirect—coordination among these various institutions to fill in gaps and correct inequities in existing programs. With these thoughts in mind, I propose that a three-pronged strategy be considered as the first stage of renewing American social insurance so that it continues to guarantee every citizen's right to basic protection from the hazards of the marketplace in an ever-changing world.

Mandatory retirement, I believe, should be eliminated, even though this will not greatly alter the trends toward earlier exits from the labor force. Far bolder and more effective would be efforts to eliminate anomalies in the treatment of older workers in job-training programs and employment practices. Only 3.1 percent of all Americans over age 65 participated in adult education programs in 1981, compared to 12.8 percent of the entire population over age 17.[20] With few exceptions, corporate training programs are geared to adapt introductory-level workers and employees under age 40 with potential to future opportunities and needs of the firm. Yet if we are to capitalize on the intellectual resources of aging workers, greater emphasis must be placed on preparing people to pursue two or three careers during their working years. Universities, vocational schools, and other postsecondary centers should try harder to recruit mature students to pursue general-education curricula and take specialized courses even if they do not matriculate for a degree.

In addition, government officials and corporate planners should facilitate older people's (re)entry into the marketplace. Public policies should encourage experiments with work programs. Surely there are better ways to solve employees' grievances than helping them to qualify for disability benefits or encouraging them to take early retirement. Work schedules and benefit packages could be adapted so as to increase the likelihood that men and women in the third quarter of life can earn money and/or increased health care protection through part-time employment. Corporate planners might profitably take cues from major corporations, such as McDonald's and the Atlantic Richfield Company, that have sought to create a climate in which both employees and employers benefit from the maturity and reliability of men and women in their seventies. These pacesetters have created job banks, job sharing, ride sharing, and flextime arrangements and have used corporate associations and newsletters to enhance their human-resource management capabilities.[21] Greater priority should be given to federally seeded volunteering and public-service initiatives, such as those already under way through the Retired Senior Volunteer Program and the Federal Senior Community Service Employment Program.

Consonant with the transgenerational features of social insurance, I would advance an even more daring idea: Why not permit workers to borrow against their future pensions in order to pay for training that might enhance their worth and longevity in the labor force? Particularly in the experimental stages of this initiative, policymakers would want to impose limits. Workers should not be permitted to take out for educational purposes more than they have already set aside for OASDHI protection. The future benefits received by people who opt for this provision will have to be based on FICA contributions adjusted for educational outlays. The merits of this revision, in my view, are worth the difficulties of implementation. Investing sensibly in the future is ultimately cheaper than compensating for past circumstances often beyond people's control. At a time of rising tuition and increased pressures on workers to upgrade their skills, this new source of money might make a difference between job burnout and career advancement. Thus, this measure serves as yet another way to bridge job training and retirement policies, with the needs and interests of middle-aged taxpayers uppermost in mind. For social insurance ideally provides a floor of protection to people continually in transition.

More than ever before, policymakers must ensure that social security really does provide an adequate basis of financial support for all Americans. As a result of the 1983 amendments, every American worker eventually will be covered under OASDHI. Having achieved this long-range goal of universal coverage, policymakers must now take steps to ensure that this objective is a genuinely meaningful achievement. The best way to proceed, I believe, is to adhere to a policy choice made before the first Title II benefit was ever paid. Reinhold Hohaus, vice president and actuary of the Metropolitan Life Insurance Company, argued in "Equity, Adequacy, and Related Factors in Old-Age Security" that the principles of "equity" had to be acknowledged in social insurance. Nevertheless, guaranteeing a "precise" relationship between contributions and benefits should be secondary to the goal of assuring "social adequacy." Hohaus believed that the first objective should be a "minimum income" which would prevent beneficiaries from "becoming a charge on society."

Have the social security amendments that began in 1939 maintained a proper balance between adequacy and equity? No definitive answer is possible. Robert J. Myers has demonstrated that 1982 benefit levels were not much above what had been anticipated under the 1939 legislation; on the other hand, there had been significant expansion beyond that intended in the 1950 amendments.[22]

From this historian's perspective, Myers's analysis should be taken a step further. Prevailing assumptions about social security entitlements are generally too pat, because most commentators ignore the temporal process in which a particular set of entitlements came into being. After all, the monthly retirement benefits to which older Americans can now lay claim are fundamentally different from the ones to which they were initially entitled in 1935 or 1939.

In the end, however, the historical record provides no clearcut basis for determining the ideal present and future relationship between the adequacy and equity of social security benefits. Nor do experiences in any other countries offer any obvious guidelines. Comparing the old-age pensions of American workers with average earnings to those of employees in a dozen advanced western European countries reveals that the U.S. falls into the intermediate range. Benefits for individuals are somewhat lower than in Europe; benefits for a married couple are somewhat higher.[23]

While historical and crosscultural analyses do not yield definitive conclusions, they do at least remind us that there is latitude for serious reflection on a wide range of alternatives. For example, I would increase Supplemental Security Income payments to guarantee that those dependents of workers with minimal covered earnings receive a benefit equal to the poverty level. The case for this revision does not depend just on historical precedent; it can be made on grounds of empirical evidence and appeals to justice. No other component of our existing retirement system will ever provide social security's universal coverage. Those who do not benefit from individual retirement accounts and other retirement vehicles tend to be those who are the poorest paid. Insofar as this nation values the work ethic—and it does—then we should be prepared to guarantee that no one who has made a contribution to America's economic growth should be denied the right to a minimal standard of living in old age.

What about those who have not earned the right to a sufficient income? The original vision of social security provides guidance. From the very beginning, assistance was deemed an integral part of the social insurance umbrella of protection. Social security benefits, tilted from the outset to provide a higher rate of return for lower-income workers, were designed to provide a measure of support to those people whose activities have not necessarily been remunerated in earnings that truly or fairly represent the value of their contributions. Existing laws, moreover, already reflect this principle, though it is mainly honored in the breach. If SSI payments and medicaid constitute the minimal standards of decency and health that this nation feels it must extend to every aged, blind, and disabled person, then no SSI beneficiary should have a "real" income that falls below the official poverty line. Achieving this objective in turn requires better coordination among various federal antipoverty measures. On the one hand, I would calculate the dollar value of food stamps and other in-kind transfers in determining a person's income needs. On the other hand, I would freeze all minimum benefits under social security enacted between 1939 and 1983 and use SSI as a "safety net" for all age groups.

Social insurance must also be adjusted to accommodate the changing status of women. Earnings-sharing should be instituted over a thirty-year period because it promotes security for the career homemaker without being unfair to the working wife. Closely tied with the implementation of this reform should be the gradual elimination of the 50-percent spousal benefit. Marriage no longer serves as a potentially universal vehicle for preventing economic adversity to a woman or man with limited employment opportunities and earnings potential. Indeed, single women—particularly those who have been divorced and widowed—have more acute needs than most married people.

Consideration also should be given to providing caregiver credits. In calculating average earnings for determining social security benefits, there should be no penalty if an individual chooses not to engage in full-time paid employment in order to care for a family member. If present trends continue, four-generation families will increasingly become the form. By the end of the century, more and more working people will be looking to nonfamilial institutions to help not just with the care of children, but also to provide meals, housekeeping, and day care arrangements for the frail elderly and other dependents. Some of these services will be purchased in the private sector; others will have to be provided by the federal government, though, in an age of fiscal austerity, the ability of the public sector to provide adequate support is questionable.[24] In this context, we must be willing to acknowledge that the care that the family members provide for one another is a time-tested, generally unpaid service that can be quite expensive to workers and taxpayers if bought in the marketplace or financed through government. Underwriting this intergenerational service through social security, therefore, is less costly than other options. Skeptics might object that providing family-care credits only in cases where relatives are assisted is unfair because it gives preferential treatment to caring for family members. I would counter by noting that such a bias is discriminatory only if the caregiver's status were in question. It is not: Decisions about such credits would be made independent of a potential beneficiary's marital status or household arrangement.

These three proposals reinforce social security's essential role as the foundation for all income security initiatives in the United States. Rather than use OASDI as a safety valve for unemployment among older workers, I am laying the foundations for a more imaginative human-resource policy. Rather than compartmentalize the adequacy and equity functions of social insurance, my recommendations seek to mesh cybernetic interactions in a more coherent manner. Rather than presume to resolve the tensions between individual rights and family responsibilities, they offer a way of providing benefits that is neutral in its treatment of marriage without undermining the crucial role families play in American society. To corroborate the social insurance principles that animate OASDHI, they emphasize that social security is an essential expression of community that at once transcends and links together generational interests. Note, however, that viewing social security as a floor for other programs frankly acknowledges the limits of any social welfare policy. These revisions, in fact, point to one overriding rule that should be followed when contemplating any social security reforms. Lawmakers henceforth should do whatever is necessary—but no more—to establish and maintain a socially acceptable level of income for all Americans.

## CONCLUSION

This package offers a balanced response to the challenges posed by developments in recent American history, but the dynamic equilibrium it hopes to achieve will be ephemeral. What is considered adequate today may be seen as a substandard program tomorrow. Any scheme that attempts to ensure fairness without substantially increasing outlays will not please everybody. The reason for this goes well beyond cost considerations or perceptions— valid or biased—that some segments of the population are benefiting from changes in the status quo more than others.

Readjusting the tension between adequacy and equity, after all, is not just a matter between the sexes. Social security's architects and reformers have been wise in not introducing differential treatment along racial or ethnic lines. And yet, we cannot be blind to the fact that the question of "social adequacy" in this country is acutely a racial and ethnic matter. Differences in black-white life expectancy at various ages put minorities at a disadvantage vis-à-vis whites throughout the life course. Efforts to establish universal coverage under social security must take account of the fact that millions of illegal Hispanic aliens are working in this country without the protection afforded by social insurance.[25] All of which is to say that we dare not allow erroneous and self-serving cliches about social security being a middle-class institution to preclude disinterested analysis of the program's long-standing "welfare" function. Insofar as social security is one of this nation's primary weapons in the continuing war against poverty, we need to assess how its various programs serve to meet the basic needs of all Americans regardless of age, gender, race, or origin.

Nevertheless, the social security revisions proposed here will not suffice in and of themselves. We cannot rely solely on the Supplemental Security Income program to ensure a floor of support because it is not our only antipoverty program. This nation has proportionately fewer children now than at any other time in its history, yet a greater percentage live in disadvantaged circumstances. Nearly half of the children born today will become eligible for child support before reaching age 16. Roughly 50 percent of all children living in female-headed households are poor; only 11 percent of the absent fathers of young Aid to Families with Dependent Children beneficiaries pay any child support.[26] Thus efforts to reform AFDC and other means-tested schemes must begin rather than end with the proposition that public assistance is linked to OASDHI. I urge that a proposal for child support insurance, developed at the Institute for Poverty Research, be tested. Under this proposal, all parents who live apart from their children are liable for a tax on their gross income for child support. This venture promises to increase the economic security of the very young while reducing case loads and welfare costs.[27] For the sake of our future— not just to placate contemporary critics—we must scrutinize benefits and services targeted across the spectrum. Only in this way can social insurance serve the young and middle-aged as well as the old in a pluralistic society.

Paradoxically, although public philosophers have been quite vociferous in debating the merits of distributive justice, Americans have been less inclined to talk about what we owe one another. "Our sense of citizenship, of social warmth, and a shared fate," comments George Will, "has become thin gruel."[28] Does this imply, at bottom, that the ideal of mutual responsibility long associated with social insurance has become so threadbare that it can be discarded as chimerical? Not at all. Neoliberals and neoconservatives alike should take their cue from Senator Bill Bradley who, in the midst of the debates over the 1983 amendments, noted that "social security is the best expression of community that we have in this country today."[29]

Under the scenario I am sketching, social security would remain a universal program and would continue to operate on a pay-as-you-go basis. But the future scope and growth of benefits depend on other developments in the political economy. Some commentators predict that it will be harder in the future to maintain the rate of return that beneficiaries have enjoyed thus far. Experts disagree, however, on the extent to which the baby boom generation may or may not get its money's worth. If by "equitable" one assumes that workers will get benefits roughly equal to their employer/employee contributions, then it appears that high-income, single male workers will not get a full return by the end of the century. Single female workers with maximum covered earnings are in a more favorable position because women tend to live longer and thus can expect to receive greater lifetime benefits. And "if the payroll taxes are increased to a sufficiently high level so that the system will be on a self-supporting basis, the failure to receive one's 'money's worth' will also apply to the average wage earner."[30] In plain English, this means that if social security is viewed as self-contained and old-age and survivors insurance is treated as if it were the only source of retirement income, then we are heading for disaster.

But such worst case forecasts very often overlook or underestimate the extent to which workers with above-average earnings in the future can—and will—rely on personal savings, IRAs, and private pension plans to supplement their OASDHI benefits. They also tend to discount the role that an expanded SSI program might play for the lower-income retiree.[31] Indeed, if we are willing to admit that macroeconomic trends will affect individuals' "equity" in the system, then we must acknowledge that the whole question of intergenerational equity is confounded by matters of capital investment and national priorities. To what degree should tomorrow's elderly benefit from future gains in productivity? To what extent should their well-being be insulated from downturns in the economy? What proportion of our country's resources should be allocated to guarantee that social security benefits are equitable and adequate? Should a limit be placed on federal expenditures? If so, how should that limit be established? As a percentage of the gross national product? A share of the current budget? These are tough questions that can only be answered satisfactorily if OAS-DHI's financial prognosis is assessed in light of other retirement vehicles. The issue of old-age security will not be adequately addressed unless we view it as an issue in which all age groups have a stake.

Treating social security as neither a covenant nor a contract, but rather as an expression of community reaffirms some of the program's most important traditional values. It underscores the system's central role in American life: No other bureaucracy is so well positioned to assure everyone regardless of race, gender, or age the financial wherewithal necessary for a minimal standard of living. At the same time, it sets an agenda which acknowledges that sustaining mutual interdependence in the American commonwealth presupposes such a shared past and a common future. For if a major function of social insurance in the United States is to promote flexibility and to maximize each person's options in a highly fluid, uncertain, and technocratically driven society, social security bears major responsibility for ensuring that fundamental protection is afforded across the public and private sectors.

Can we afford such compassion in the name of justice? Yes— but let us be honest and admit that our humanitarian impulse works to our enlightened advantage. As a people we consider it to be in our national interest to spend billions on defense and to rebuild roads and bridges. Does it not make as much sense to allocate funds to revitalize our human resources? Are we not protecting ourselves by promoting "welfare" in the true sense of the term?

The meaning of community embodied in OASDHI is fragile indeed. We cannot depend on it, yet we cannot live as a nation without it. As a people, we must constantly renew our affirmation of perduring values while we reshape this enduring social institution to meet basic national objectives. How we treat our fellow citizens and our future selves under the principle of social insurance thus mirrors, for better or worse, what we take to be the essential quality and tenor of American life.

## NOTES

1. This chapter first appeared in *Fifty Years of Social Security: Past Achievements and Future Challenges*, an information paper (99–70) prepared for use by the Special Committee on Aging, U.S. Senate (Washington, D.C.: Government Printing Office, 1985). The publication was released to coincide with a special hearing of the Special Committee on Aging held in Pittsburgh on August 13, 1985. The editor and the author wish to express their appreciation to the committee and to Senator John Heinz, the committee chairman, for permission to reprint this essay here.

2. For more on this theme, see W. Andrew Achenbaum, *Social Security: Visions and Revisions* (New York: Cambridge University Press, 1986).

3. Richard Lowitt and Maurinne Beasley, eds., *One Third of a Nation: Lorena Hickok Reports on the Great Depression* (Urbana: University of Illinois Press, 1981), p. 169; "Old Age Pensions," *Encyclopedia of the Social Sciences*, vol. 11 (New York: Macmillan Company, 1937), pp. 456–57.

4. Robert S. McElvaine, ed., *Down and Out in the Great Depression* (Chapel Hill: University of North Carolina Press, 1983), pp. 84, 100, 108.

5. Staff of the Committee on Economic Security, *Social Security in America* (Washington, D.C.: U.S. Government Printing Office, 1937); Committee on Finance, *The Economic Security Act* (Washington, D.C.: Government Printing Office, 1935), p. 1337.

6. *Congressional Record*, June 10, 1939, p. 6964.

7. J. Douglas Brown, "Economic Problems in the Provision of Security Againt Life Hazards of Workers," *American Economic Review* 30 (March 1940), p. 67; Frank Bane, "Social Security Expands," *Social Service Review* 13 (December 1939), pp. 608–9.

8. *Report of the Advisory Council on Social Security*, December 10, 1938, p. 18.

9. John Kenneth Galbraith, *The Affluent Society* (Boston: Houghton Mifflin, 1958), p. 115.

10. Edwin L. Dale, "The Security of Social Security: The Young Pay for the Old," *New York Times Magazine*, January 14, 1973, pp. 8, 45.

11. For a classic demonstration of this point, see Ida C. Merriam, "Young Adults and Social Security," *Social Security Bulletin* 31 (August 1968), p. 3.

12. Marie L. Dallach, "Old Age American Style," *New Outlook*, vol. 162 (October 1933), p. 50; see also, Warren S. Thompson and P. K. Whelpton, "A Nation of Elders in the Making," *American Mercury* 19 (April 1930), pp. 392–95.

13. Joseph A. Califano, Jr., *Governing America: An Insider's View of the White House and the Cabinet* (New York: Simon and Schuster, 1981), p. 398; Robert J. Samuelson, "Busting the Budget: The Graying of America," *National Journal*, February 18, 1978, pp. 259–60; and Robert B. Hudson, "The Graying of the Federal Budget and Its Consequences for Old-Age Policy," *The Gerontologist* 18 (October 1978), pp. 428–40.

14. National Commission on Social Security Reform, Memorandum no. 13, "Surveys of Public Confidence as to Financial Status of the Social Security Program," April 7, 1982. A more recent survey confirms these results. See "A Fifty-Year Report Card on the Social Security System: The Attitudes of the American Public," American Association of Retired Persons, August 1985.

What made this pattern all the more disturbing is that it paralleled a longer trend of popular disenchantment with governmental effectiveness. Public opinion polls had documented a dramatic decline, beginning in 1964, in Americans' trust in government. Surprisingly, the steepest drop was registered among those over the age of 65. See Harold Johnson et al., *American Values and the Elderly* (Ann Arbor: Institute of Gerontology, 1979), p. S–64.

15. Quoted in "Members of Congress and Aides Seeking Ways to Keep Social Security Solvent," *New York Times*, January 2, 1981, p. A11.

16. Philip Longman, "Taking America to the Cleaners," *Washington Monthly* 14 (1982), p. 26.

17. Nancy Foner, *Ages in Conflict* (New York: Columbia University Press, 1984).

18. J. Douglas Brown, *Essays on Social Security* (Princeton: Industrial Relations Section, 1977), appendix, p. 47.

19. "Reagan Signs Social Security Changes into Law," *New York Times*, April 21, 1983, p. 9.

20. Evelyn P. Kay, *Participation in Adult Education, 1981* (Washington, D.C.: National Center for Education Statistics, 1982), p. 6.

21. Select Committee on Aging, House of Representatives, *New Business Perspectives on the Older Worker* (Washington, D.C.: Government Printing Office, 1981), pp. 56–67; "Corporate Employee Relations. Making the Right Decision," internal Arco pamphlet, 1982.

22. Robert J. Myers, *Social Security* (Homewood, Ill., Richard D. Irwin, 1981), pp. 261–63; Memorandum no. 33, dated June 30, 1982, for the National Commission on Social Security Reform.

23. Max Horlick, "The Earnings Replacement Rate of Old-Age Benefits: An International Comparison," *Social Security Bulletin* 33 (March 1970), pp. 3–16.

24. George Masnick and Mary Jo Bane, *The Nation's Families* (Boston: Auburn House Publishing Company, 1980); Joseph Califano, "The Four-Generation Family," *Annals of the American Academy of Political and Social Science* 438 (1978), pp. 96–107; Ethel Shanas, "The Family As a Social Support in Old Age," *The Gerontologist* 19 (1979), pp. 169–74.

25. 1971 White House Conference on Aging, *Final Report, Volume II* (Washington, D.C.: Government Printing Office, 1973), pp. 177–96; Gayle B. Thompson, "Blacks and Social Security Benefits: Trends, 1960–73," *Social Security Bulletin* 40 (1977), pp. 30–40; Julian Abbott, "Socioeconomic Characteristics of the Elderly: Some Black-White Differences," *Social Security Bulletin* 40 (1977), pp. 16–42; Reynolds Farley, *A Narrowing Gap* (Cambridge, Mass.: Harvard University Press, 1985).

26. Alan Pifer, "Perceptions of Childhood and Youth," *Annual Report Essays* (New York: Carnegie Corporation, 1983), pp. 157–67; U.S. Department of Health and Human Services, *Child Support Enforcement* (Washington, D.C.: Government Printing Office, 1985), pp. 18, 28; Samuel H. Preston, "Children and the Elderly in the United States," *Scientific American* 251 (1984), pp. 44–49; Committee on Ways and Means, *Children in Poverty* (Washington, D.C.: Government Printing Office, 1985).

27. Irwin Garfinkel, "The Role of Child Support Insurance in Antipoverty Policy," *Annals of the American Academy of Political and Social Science* 479 (May 1985), pp. 119–31.

28. George F. Will, *Statecraft as Soulcraft* (New York: Simon and Schuster, 1983), p. 45.

29. *Congressional Record* 129 (March 24, 1983), p. S4098.

30. Robert J. Myers, "Money's Worth Comparison for Social Security Benefits," NCSSR memorandum 45, August 12, 1982, p. 5; Sylvester Schieber, *Preserving Social Security* (Washington, D.C.: Employment Benefits Research Institute, 1982), pp. 29–30; Carolyn Weaver, *The Crisis in Social Security* (Durham, N.C.: Duke University Press, 1982), pp. 188–89.

31. Alicia H. Munnell, *The Future of Social Security* (Washington, D.C.: Brookings Institution, 1977), p. 58.

# 7

# Social Security in 1995:
# The Future as a Reflection
# of the Past

WILBUR J. COHEN

I begin a reflection on the future with thoughts of the past. For me, the future of social security cannot be divorced from the broad cycles of social reform that have affected this country's history. But, I must also consider social security in personal terms. After all, I have spent fifty-one years talking and writing about the same subject. Although different administrations have come to Washington and the circumstances surrounding social legislation reform have changed, I would like to think that the broad objectives—and the general means of reaching them—have remained the same.

I come from Wisconsin, and I consider myself lucky to have inherited some of the intellectual tradition of that state. In particular, I regard myself as a disciple of John R. Commons and Edwin Witte, both of whom taught at the University of Wisconsin, where the institutional economists believed in moderating the excesses of capitalism through a free-market system tempered by the existence of unions and government. On the one hand, they wished to retain the flexibility of the free market; on the other hand, they wanted to control the excesses of industrialization and urbanization.

As for my theory of history, I take my text from the Schlesingers, senior and junior, who have propounded a cyclical theory of social reform and social legislation. Complex factors related to the business cycle, the evolution of political parties, and the public's tolerance for experiment provide the engine that drives this cycle. In this brief summary, I must necessarily simplify some of the complexity in order to outline the development of American social welfare programs in bold relief.

This century began with an underdeveloped public sector in America. The institutional landscape was devoid of such now fundamentally accepted programs as workers' compensation, unemployment compensation, and social security. Only in 1905 did the country take the first tentative steps toward a program of social insurance. It took those steps in ways consistent with the political and constitutional outlook of the era. That implied that social legislation would arrive on the state level before it reached the federal level. Indeed, workers' compensation, the first major social insurance program, took the form of separate state programs that were enacted in a series of laws that stretched from the beginning of the century until 1948. These laws left a great deal to be desired, and the flaws can still be detected today. Rehabilitation, provisions for retraining, and coverage of occupational diseases still remain inadequate in many of the state compensation laws. Yet workers' compensation, for all of its flaws, provided an important experience on which we were able to build. We based much of social security disability insurance and Supplemental Security Income on our experience with workers' compensation. In a similar manner, mothers' pension laws, first enacted in the state of Illinois in 1910, served as a model for Aid to Dependent Children in the Social Security Act of 1935.

What happened on the federal level during the first great period of twentieth-century social reform? One important legacy was the Pure Food and Drug Act, an act which even the Reagan administration does not seem to want to dismantle. Solidly based on the federal government's power to regulate interstate commerce, this act has proved to be an enduring form of the government's regulation of industry. I speak from experience. When I was secretary of Health, Education, and Welfare, I came to realize the important power that this law placed in the agency's hands.

Other innovations in the federal sector paved the way for future social reform, even though they were not directly related to social welfare. The modern income tax, which dates from 1913, provided a means for the federal government to collect revenue from a broad base of its citizens, thereby facilitating our later efforts to implement social welfare programs. Further, the Federal Reserve Act of 1913 provided a means of stabilizing the banking and monetary system, another prerequisite for the establishment of a large social insurance system.

We tend to dismiss the creation of the Children's Bureau (in 1912) and the Women's Bureau (in 1920) as important social reforms, yet they were vitally important. These agencies established the principle of collecting data to determine the need for social reform. The need was urgent. Even at the beginning of the depression decade of the thirties, for example, this nation still lacked reliable statistics on unemployment. Agencies such as the Children's Bureau and the Women's Bureau helped to fill in some of the gaps in the nation's statistical information. As such, they performed work that formed an important prelude to the events of the New Deal.

All of these various state and federal programs were products of the progressive era; one could highlight the year 1905 as the beginning of the great outpouring of social concern that led to the creation of the programs. Then, with the exception of the Sheppard-Towner Act (1921–1929) and other isolated acts of social reform, the nation entered the downside of the cycle. The pace of social reform slowed during the 1920s.

The crisis of the depression awakened our slumbering social conscience and produced a torrent of social legislation. This second great wave of reform included the 1935 passage of the Social Security Act. This act, which I might with some justification call the most important piece of domestic legislation ever enacted in the United States, included ten different programs, all of which still exist. Then, in 1938, came the passage of the Fair Labor Standards Act that established the first national minimum wage, the norm of the forty-hour working week, the precedent of overtime pay for hours beyond that, and standards for child labor. The abolition of child labor had been one of the most poignant omissions of progressive reform. Many of my late associates, such as Elizabeth Brandeis (with the help of Josephine Goldmark), had made it one of the central concerns of their lives. The Fair Labor Standards Act helped to close the circle of social reform as it realized the aspirations of progressive reformers and enacted at the federal level what so many had struggled to achieve at the state level.

If the first wave of social reform began around 1905 and the second around 1935, one would have anticipated the crest of another wave around 1965. Lyndon Johnson's Great Society arrived just on schedule and produced another extraordinary moment in our nation's history, one that included amendments to the Social Security Act that began an ambitious program of health insurance (medicare and medicaid).

By my schedule, the next round of social reform should begin around 1995, which is the reason I have chosen to highlight it in this essay. At this point, I should reiterate my faith in the existence of this cycle, my belief that these various reform periods are not random events but rather reflections of what might be called a Kondratieff cycle of social reform. A number of factors explain the existence of this cycle and make me confident that it will still operate in 1995. In the first place, I believe that not everything gets done during each of the reform periods. Despite people's desires and their perceptions of social needs, a certain exhaustion and impatience takes hold. People begin to believe that reform costs too much, poses too many administrative difficulties. They therefore shy away from the completion of the agenda, but the agenda remains in place. Even Mr. Reagan has begun to discover the limits of what David Stockman has termed the Reagan revolution. He now sees that people get bored by what the federal government wants to do and that people at some point do not want to pay the actual or social costs of what they think needs to be done. Then, too, the participants in the social process do not remain in place. Members of Congress wish to become governors, and the governors want to run for senator. Repeated over fifty states and 3,000 counties, this process of political change soon takes its toll, and the moment of consensus that permits great social programs soon slips away. So it was for Presidents Theodore Roosevelt and Lyndon Johnson; so it will be for President Reagan. In short, a cycle governs society's affairs that limits how much can be done at any one time and leaves important things for the next generation to do.

For me, this cycle has a very personal meaning. I would like to think that I have helped to advance the items on President Franklin

Roosevelt's agenda, both at the time and during the Great Society. I also know that I have left many things for future generations to accomplish. When I came to Washington as a young man in 1934, one of my friends was Abraham Epstein, who was famous for his advocacy of old-age pensions in the twenties on behalf of such fraternal groups as the Eagles. And he and I would have these deep discussions in which we would prod each other: Each of us would try to incite the other to do more. So, one day, when we got into a heated discussion, he said, "Well your trouble, Wilbur, is that you don't want to leave anything for your grandchildren to do." I have remembered that line. I now have four grandchildren, and I believe I have left them a lot to do.

My hopes for my grandchildren sustain me in this low period in the trough of the cycle when antigovernment, antiexpenditure, and antiprogram attitudes seem to predominate. In my opinion, this day will end because the unrelenting forces of industrialization, unemployment, sickness, ill health, and disability have not been in any way postponed by the budget or the deficit. They remain with us, and they will probably get worse.

When the next cycle of reform arrives, what will happen? I believe that medicare will be extended to provide long-term care. Nursing home care has already become one of the great social needs of our time, yet it will take some sort of crisis to force the issue. Then people—particularly the children of the aged—will come to see the costs involved in providing long-term care. At present the median cost hovers around $2,000 a month for minimal care, which amounts to little more than custodial care. Better quality care runs to $3,000 a month. If we assume for the sake of argument that the average stay in a nursing home lasts two years, the costs reach $60,000 and more. Looking toward 1995, I see the makings of a movement to finance these costs through social insurance. Secretary of Health and Human Services Bowen has already spoken of catastrophic coverage of in-patient hospitalization, but I think he fails to give notice to the highest priority. Few people, I believe, need to spend six months in a hospital; instead, they require a different sort of care. Yet when they enter a nursing home, they put themselves in great financial peril. Nor does the peril end there. One of the most compelling catastrophes that we see is a man or woman who has to divorce his or her spouse in order to become needy enough to qualify for medicaid. What sort of family policy is that?

In the next ten to twenty years, the crisis in long-term care will reach a crescendo, and in the next cycle of reform something will be done to remedy the situation. Financing nursing home care will not be enough. We also need to find substitutes for institutional care, such as home health services, homemaker services, and supportive social services. Such substitutes should enable people to stay out of a nursing home, which is a worthy goal in itself, or to rehabilitate themselves enough to live in congregate housing or a quasi-retirement home. In other words, long-term care must come to mean more than the present-day custodial nursing home care. We require an array of options to get the right person in the right setting at the right time with the right services. This requirement implies a need for a tremendous amount of high-quality specialized services, which will cost a great deal. I believe that we need to protect an individual against those costs through some form of insurance.

The public sector need not assume the entire burden. Perhaps some combination of responsibilities between the public and private sectors would be appropriate similar to the way we handled medicare. In fact, we are in a much better position to use the social security system to pay for services today than we were in 1965. And by 1995 I estimate that people will have an average of $500 to $600 a month through social security; if they enter a nursing home that costs $2000 a month, they will have $500 of their own income to use to help pay for the nursing home. Perhaps we could work out in some truly pragmatic fashion a way to take care of the residual. Therefore, although we may fuss at the cost, I doubt we will allow our parents and grandparents to die without doing something to take care of them in their later years, nor will we violate our traditions and put all the costs on the children.

Let me emphasize again the role of the private sector. I envision a whole new complex of home health services, hospice services, and retirement homes and villages, and I believe a tremendous opportunity exists for the private sector to provide some of them. For example, the Upjohn Company already is heavily involved in homemaker services. I would hope that many other providers would enter the field in what would be a truly creative and productive relationship between the public and private sectors.

Even if we find a means to finance these new services through medicare, that does not mean we can neglect medicaid. After all, half of medicaid's expenditures are dedicated to nursing home care. Furthermore, the states bear half of the medicaid cost, and I see a difficult time ahead for state government. Part of my vision stems from my residence in Texas, which has made me very sensitive to the changing nature of the state revenue bases. Beyond Texas, the entire nation will have to cope with less revenue from the federal government, particularly if we follow the logic of the Gramm-Rudman bill. I believe that within a few years these factors will combine and produce a crisis in medicaid that could well end with medicaid's being federalized. Then medicaid might be transformed into some sort of national health insurance program.

That brings me to one of the concerns that has been with me throughout my career. If I were to have any say, this country would enact, as part of the next great wave of reform, some form of health insurance to cover the entire population. The lack of universal health insurance may be the single most glaring gap in our social welfare system, the one that I most regret leaving to my grandchildren. Our lack of health insurance has repercussions that extend to our entire social welfare system. It helps to explain, for example, why welfare is mounting since mothers hesitate to go off the rolls for fear of losing medicaid coverage for their children. I confess that I find it difficult to blame such people who have been forced to stay on the welfare rolls because of the faulty design of our social welfare system.

At the same time, I do not think that the country will enact a health insurance measure of the type that I have often advocated. That is because time has made many of our health insurance proposals, such as the Wagner-Murray-Dingell bill, the Truman bill, the Corman bill, and the Kennedy bill, obsolete. We now have about 85 percent of the population covered by some form of health insurance. The quality of that insurance varies, I realize, and it also fluctuates with the unemployment rate. As people lose their jobs, they often face a period of great risk in which medicaid offers the only solution, and even medicaid may be impossible to obtain (as in the case of a prime aged male with no dependents who is out of work). Despite these problems, I believe that the country will move toward a "mandated" plan rather than the sort of plan I have advocated for fifty years. I remain convinced that mine is the better plan, yet the public appears to demand choice in their form of health insurance. Americans prefer a patchwork, fragmented plan rather than a universal, uniform plan. Therefore, I think we will move to a Canadian style of health insurance, perhaps on a state-by-state basis or perhaps with a federal law, similar to the unemployment insurance law. Such a law would require employers to provide health insurance, and we would blanket in the remaining population (perhaps 10 percent) by paying the cost out of earmarked income or general revenues.

Having taken these measures, we would arrive in 1995 with everyone having some form of public or private health insurance from the day they are born until the day that they die. I think the nation will take the necessary steps to reach this point because of improvements in the ability of medicine to prolong life. It is now possible to do things that were beyond the realm of possibility when my mother died in 1941. Faced with a similar situation today, people will not let their concern over cost override their desire to see their family members receive the benefits of modern technology. In the final analysis, the body politic will accede to health insurance because the aging of the population and medicine's technological achievements will make health care one of society's highest priorities.

When I survey developments in social security, I like to also use the term "safety net." When someone uses the term social security, most people think he is referring only to old-age, survivors, disability, and hospital insurance (OASDHI) and not to the other components of the Social Security Act. But, in the year 1995, we will need to look beyond issues in health care in order to face the social crises of the day. Other parts of the safety net, such as unemployment compensation, will require attention.

Simply put, we need a better unemployment insurance system. We have arrived in an age where full employment is taken to mean an unemployment rate as high as 6 percent. I grew up in an era when Leon Keyserling and other economists were reluctant to accept 4 percent unemployment as full employment. Apparently, however, we have accepted 6 and even 7 or 8 percent unemployment as a natural part of the free-market system in which people move from job to job and families contain two earners. Our unemployment compensation system, far from reflecting the labor market of the future, does not even reflect the labor market of today. We continue to have fifty different, disorganized, and disoriented state systems, each of which rests on its own bottom. I think such a system is ludicrous. Furthermore, a crisis already exists within these state systems. Unemployment compensation is one social security program that is going bankrupt, and no one hardly ever mentions it. During the past ten years, the states have had to borrow billions of dollars from the federal government to sustain the system: first with no-interest loans and then from the general revenues. This borrowing only exacerbates the federal deficit. I would place a high priority on some modernization of the unemployment insurance system.

This problem is one of long-standing interest to me as one might expect of a boy from Wisconsin, which passed the first state unemployment compensation law in the nation. I returned to this problem fairly recently when President Carter asked me to chair the National Commission on Unemployment Compensation. The administration of President Reagan paid absolutely no attention to the three years of research that went into this report, and the Congress has chosen to ignore the recommendations made by the commission, even though they are broadly representative of labor, management, and the public. What has caused this myopia? Perhaps Gresham's Law has operated in the social welfare field: the hysterical crisis over OASDHI financing has driven out discussion of the real crisis in unemployment compensation.

I do not think we will be able to ignore the crisis from now until 1995. We will need a strengthened employment service to meet the high technology crisis; we will have to reform our financing of unemployment insurance. When we do so, we will have to examine the structure of the American family very carefully. The present system has rested on the same premise since 1935: A man works and a woman stays at home. Benefits were paid as though the man were the only breadwinner. Changed circumstances compel a comprehensive revision of the program.

The other program that requires revision is our welfare program.

I think that ten years from now a true safety net will exist under-
neath the many programs already in place. The nation presently
maintains what I would describe as a partial safety net that includes, for example, Aid to Families with Dependent Children,
food stamps, and WIC (Special Supplemental Food Program for
Women, Infants, and Children). This partial safety net is riddled
with holes. Not adequate for most welfare recipients, it fails totally
in the case of people who fall through it. To cite only the most
obvious example, we have no national program to meet the needs
of a poor person who does not have children and who is not old,
blind, or disabled, yet many poor people fall into this category.

As I make these suggestions, I am aware that I am writing in
the middle of one of the most conservative decades this nation has
ever experienced. I realize that people may sympathize with my
desires but may also despair over the nation's ability to pay for
the programs that will translate them into reality. I confess that if
I were presenting these proposals to Congress, I would come prepared with a cost-specific plan. Whenever I think about social
reform, I remember former Senator Carl Curtis who always asked
me how much a particular proposal would cost and how I proposed
to pay for it. In this context, I do not wish to answer Senator
Curtis's questions directly but rather to indicate my sense of the
future course of the economy.

I part company with those who take a pessimistic view of the
future of the American economy. These people suggest that the
nation will soon stagger under the burdens of dependency: They
argue, for example, that social security will soon go broke because
of the ratio of the working to the nonworking population. It seems
to me that these nay-sayers lack a historical imagination. It is as
if they are mired in the mentality of 1931, unable to see beyond
the Great Depression. This same mentality characterizes those
people who suggest that the doldrums of the seventies and eighties
will remain with us forever and that the nation will continue to
suffer from low productivity.

I take another view. Technology may launch the greatest expansion of productivity between 1990 and 2020 that this nation has
ever witnessed. In other words, I take a cyclical view of the economy similar to my cyclical theory of social reform. Periods of
expansion and periods of recession alternate, but the general trend

has been upward. As a result, I have had greater opportunities than did my father, and he had more opportunity than did his father. I believe that future generations may well see higher standards of living and a better quality of life than I have seen.

My view of the economy makes me sanguine about the future of social security. Although some worry about the ratio of workers to retirees, I can imagine a world in which the workers produce many times what they do today. That will mean that we are able to do more for less, such as funding the retirement of the baby boom with a lower percentage of workers in the general population.

No one needs to tell me that my views run contrary to the conventional wisdom of the moment. Here again I take comfort in the historical view and in my own history. Let me pose a hypothetical situation. If I had told you in 1932 that we would have medicare, medicaid, and social security in 1980, you might well have replied, "impossible, fantastic, and unreal." One's view of the future, in other words, depends upon the location of one's base line. Today's greatest difficulty lies in the fact that people wish to establish the year 1980 as their base line and project the bleak economy of 1980 into the future. I do not think such a choice is wise.

I remember a discussion that took place during my childhood in Milwaukee in which I said to one of my friends, with some exasperation, "Oh, go fly to the moon." In my lifetime, someone did fly to the moon. That sort of creativity, I would like to believe, may well manifest itself in the social welfare field; the same genius of invention that we associate with business and enterprise may soon be focused on reinforcing the social safety net so as to improve the quality of the nation's life in 1995.

That will not happen unless we do a better job in the education of the young. They have to understand that the laws of probability apply to them as well as to the rest of us so that they do not reach old age and lament the fact that they failed to save more when they were young. I notice that when I suggest that my own students invest more in an IRA or private health insurance, they reply, "I'm not sick, and retirement is a long way off. Besides, I want to visit Spain next year." Imbued with that attitude, students have a difficult time appreciating the accomplishments of social security;

they do not understand how much the social security program has taken off their backs for the financial care of their parents.

Today's students have attitudes that sharply diverge from the ones with which I grew up in Milwaukee. As the oldest son, I took for granted the fact that I would care for my mother and father should they reach a state of dependency. When I was seventeen or eighteen, I understood that such were the ways of the world. In my lifetime, we have seen the advent of social security which has relieved sons and daughters of the major costs of dependency. That has left workers in their productive years with more income for themselves, with more money to send their children to college. In this manner, social security has served as one of the biggest federal aids to higher education that this country has ever seen. Social security has, therefore, freed the family to invest in the future by liberating it from some of the debts of the past. That may well be the greatest contribution of social security during the first fifty years of its existence.

So I face the future in an optimistic frame of mind. I firmly believe that the United States has the potential, the economic resources, and the executive and managerial abilities to fashion a better social safety net. We will build the safety net of the future on the lessons of the past. That will mean a combination of public and private responsibility; that will mean a system that sometimes sacrifices efficiency for freedom of choice; and that will mean an incremental and piecemeal approach to social policy. We will arrive at the year 1995 not only with a greater degree of productivity and an increased standard of living but with an improved social safety net as well. A lifetime of watching the cycles of social reform and a career spent designing and improving our social security programs enable me to conclude this essay on a note of impatient satisfaction: proud of the first fifty years of social security, impatient to reach the next wave of social reform, and confident that this next wave is just in sight, ready to carry America forward.

# 8

# A Reply to Wilbur J. Cohen

## ROBERT J. MYERS

This matter of looking ahead only ten years is really rather easy. As an actuary at the Social Security Administration, I have had the experience of looking far into the future. An example from the very earliest years of the social security program helps to illustrate this point.

In 1934 and 1935, when Wilbur and I first started to work on the program, the actuaries made year-by-year projections out to that far distant year, 1980, which was forty-five years in the future. Perhaps by good chance, perhaps by looking at the right estimates, we did one thing quite well. We estimated back then that the cost of the program in 1980 would be about 9.5 percent of taxable payroll. The actual cost of the old-age and survivors insurance (OASI) program, which is comparable to what was originally enacted, turned out to be within one tenth of one percent of that original estimate. The dollar figures looked very different, but, as Wilbur and I have learned over the years, one should properly look at the cost figures as percentages of taxable payroll, not in terms of dollars.

Although Wilbur and I do not share a background as actuaries, we agree on many, many things. For the purpose of this essay, however, I would like rather to examine our disagreements.

Wilbur proposes a very interesting theory of thirty-year cycles in social reform. As an actuary, I cannot go along with him. Mathematicians like to fit curves to sets of data and to project the future on the basis of an elegant curve. One never knows, however, just where the data will lead. The thirty-year cycle may work out, but then again it may not. On the other hand, it would be foolish to predict that the future is going to be exactly like what we are experiencing today. We will just have to wait until 1995 to see if Wilbur's cycle operates, or whether it may be better to use "a random walk theory" in contemplating social change.

Now let me deal with some of Wilbur's specific points. His first major theme concerned long-term care. I agree that, with the aging of the population and on the basis of my past projections and the current projections of the Social Security Administration actuaries, there is little question that the demand for long-term care will rise in the future. Not only are more people going to be age 65 and over, but higher percentages of that population are going to be at the oldest ages, where long-term nursing or other types of long-term care will become necessary. However, I cannot agree with Wilbur's prediction that this problem will be handled by medicare.

As a cautious actuary, I do not believe that long-term custodial care is an insurable risk. Its availability as an "insured right" introduces what may be called a moral-hazard problem because its use is greatly subject to an individual's preferences and actions; it cannot be administered on the basis of objective medical determinations. In other words, I think that many people would be glad to exchange their present living conditions for those in a very fine nursing home (as I hope the nursing homes of the future will be), if there were no cost-sharing provisions in the program, or if the cost-sharing could easily be met out of the OASDI benefit. In other words, long-term care insurance leaves entirely too much up to the option of the individuals covered. It would be like paying substantial unemployment insurance benefits to people who voluntarily left their jobs.

I do not think that a perfect solution to the long-term care problem exists. It may instead be a matter of picking the least worst alternative. I believe that the solution may lie in medicaid, although not the present program. Instead, we need a medicaid program with more liberal and equitable conditions; as we know and as Wilbur pointed out, some things about the present program just do not make sense. We have to look closely, for example, at the spend-down provisions, under which people have to exhaust all of their resources before they become eligible. If a couple has assets, such as a home, they should be allowed to maintain it during their lifetimes. At the end of that time, however, it does not seem appropriate for the children to inherit the assets and share in the accumulated wealth if governmental funds have been paying for the long-term care of the parents. Also, safeguards should be developed in order to prevent people from disposing of their assets (to their children or otherwise) in anticipation of receiving medicaid benefits for long-term custodial nursing-home care.

At the same time, I also believe that medicare has a role to play in long-term care. In particular, there could be improved and expanded home health services under medicare. Unlike custodial long-term care, home health services are, I believe, an insurable risk that should be looked at closely.

Wilbur next mentioned the topic of national health insurance or, as he might have it, a national health service. As he realizes, we are not going to have an ambitious, government-staffed health insurance program. I do not even see a mandated plan in the future, either on the state or federal level. We will instead continue to develop a fragmented system based on the consumer's right to choose, perhaps backed up by a better medicaid program. Furthermore, I do not agree that a single monolithic plan would necessarily be more efficient than the present complicated system under which people have all sorts of choices. I prefer this competition and variety to the possibility of a single, government-controlled plan.

As to unemployment insurance and the matter of the unemployment rate, I think that the unemployment rate is not something as easily measureable as mortality rates or even disability rates. The definition of unemployment can vary, depending upon the particular social and economic climate. Permit me a personal example. When I went back into federal service in 1981 and left my consulting business, the net effect was an increase in unemployment of one, because my move left my secretary without a job.

What about the financing of unemployment insurance? I think that it is a shame that, as Wilbur correctly notes, the state plans have become bankrupt and not much is being done about it. In this time of economic prosperity, the unemployment insurance tax rate should be much higher, so as to pay off all of the loans from the general treasury to the various state systems.

We now turn to my first love—old-age, survivors, and disability insurance. Here I must chide Wilbur on one thing. His essay repeats a very common fallacy: In the future, according to this fallacy, there will be only two workers for every retired worker under OASDI, thus making future costs unmanageable. The statement is wrong, and it does harm because it scares people about the future of the social security system. People naturally worry about two workers having to support a retired worker in addition to their own families. In reality, this figure compares workers and OASI beneficiaries (i.e., including spouses and children of aged and disabled workers and survivors of deceased workers and retirees). If the comparison were to match active and retired workers, the ratio would ultimately be more like 3 to 1, compared with the 4.5 to 1 ratio we have now.

Finally, let me change places with Wilbur and describe my vision of the social security program in the next ten years. This exercise cannot be strictly actuarial because sometimes one's wishes guide one's predictions. Objectively, however, I see relatively few changes being made to alter the very significant 1983 amendments. Most people, I believe, want to let the matter rest. I think that a few incremental changes might be made. For example, I contemplate more encouragement (or less discouragement) of continued employment after age 65. I would, therefore, increase the so-called delayed retirement credits so that they would be close to the actuarial equivalent of 8 percent per year, just as present law will do in the year 2009. I believe that this change would create more equitable treatment of people who work beyond age 65.

Incremental changes could also be made in connection with two-worker families. In theory, I support the earnings-sharing proposals which are widely made; in practice, I think that such proposals present more problems of implementation than they offer solutions to present dilemmas. Real problems exist in this area, but many of them could be greatly alleviated by incremental changes within the system.

The most important thing to do in OASI is to prevent the huge buildup of funds that will occur in the late 1980s and certainly in the 1990s. This buildup derives from two sources: the tax rates, which are to be increased in 1988 and again in 1990, and the fact that the period from 1990 to roughly 2010 will be a relatively low-cost period for the system.

The annual numbers of births in this country between 1925 and 1939 were lower than the numbers before 1925 and the numbers after 1939. As a result, we are entering a period when the population in the retirement ages, despite improved chances for survival, will likely level off. Certainly, the ratio of the population over age 65 to the working-age population will decrease. With those demographic trends, the present schedule of tax-rate increases, and the absence of economic catastrophe, conditions are ripe for the development of very large balances in the trust fund.

I think that this situation would be bad from an economic standpoint and from a political standpoint. Although we can do nothing about the demographic situation, we do have power over the tax rates. Therefore, Congress should, in my opinion, postpone the tax-rate increase scheduled for 1990 and, depending on conditions in the Hospital Insurance Trust Fund, look carefully into the possibility of lowering the overall tax rate for OASDI and HI combined.

True to my actuarial training, I look forward not only at the next ten years but also at the next fifty years. I see an OASDI system that closely resembles the one we have today. There may be some changes made, such as an increase in the retirement age. Certainly, the dollar figures of benefit amounts, maximum taxable earnings, and so on, will be different. However, let me be quite clear on one thing: The general structure of an earnings-related system with weighted benefits for lower paid people and with supplements for dependents will still be here fifty years from now. Social security, which recently celebrated its fiftieth birthday, can look forward to many future birthday parties. And, along with Wilbur, I hope to attend just as many as I can.

# Recommended Reading

Aaron, Henry J., *Economic Effects of Social Security* (Washington, D.C.: Brookings Institution, 1982).

Achenbaum, W. Andrew, *Social Security: Visions and Revisions* (New York: Cambridge University Press, 1986).

Altmeyer, Arthur J., *The Formative Years of Social Security* (Madison: University of Wisconsin Press, 1966).

Ball, Robert M., *Social Security: Today and Tomorrow* (New York: Columbia University Press, 1978).

Berkowitz, Edward D., and Kim McQuaid, *Creating the Welfare State* (New York: Praeger Publishers, 1980).

Cohen, Wilbur J., *Retirement Policies Under Social Security* (Berkeley and Los Angeles: University of California Press, 1958).

Committee on Economic Security, *Social Security in America* (Washington, D.C.: Government Printing Office, 1937).

Derthick, Martha, *Policymaking for Social Security* (Washington, D.C.: Brookings Institution, 1979).

Light, Paul, *Artful Work* (New York: Random House, 1985).

Lubove, Roy, *Struggle for Social Security* (Cambridge, Mass.: Harvard University Press, 1968).

Munnell, Alicia H., *The Future of Social Security* (Washington, D.C.: Brookings Institution, 1977).

Myers, Robert J., *Social Security*, 3d ed. (Homewood, Ill.: Richard D. Irwin, 1985).

Nelson, Daniel, *Unemployment Insurance* (Madison: University of Wisconsin Press, 1969).
Patterson, James T., *America's Struggle Against Poverty* (Cambridge, Mass.: Harvard University Press, 1981).
Stone, Deborah, *The Disabled State* (Philadelphia: Temple University Press, 1984).
Weaver, Carolyn L., *The Crisis in Social Security* (Durham, N.C.: Duke University Press, 1982).
Witte, Edwin E., *The Development of the Social Security Act* (Madison: University of Wisconsin Press, 1962).

# Index

Administrative law judges (ALJs), 111
Advisory council (1937), 61–73
Advisory council (1938), 127
Advisory council (1947–1948), 20
*Affluent Society* (Galbraith), 123
Aid to Families with Dependent Children (AFDC), 12, 134, 150
Altmeyer, Arthur, 4, 6, 58, 59, 64, 68; on Congress, 41–42; memoir by, 30; on reserve fund use, 63; before Senate finance committee, 61
American Association of Retired Persons(AARP), 13
Armstrong, Barbara, 37

Baby boom generation, 12–15, 24, 126; benefits to, 135; in retirement, 91; retirement costs to, 83; tax burden on, 92–93
Ball, Robert, 3–4, 5, 7–8, 22, 56
Beneficiaries, 113, 122–23, 124
Benefits: as asset, 88; borrowing against, 129–30; to children, 69–70; computation of, 104–5; indexation of, 86; inequality of, 65–67; levels of, 80; payment increases, 113; rates, 81–82; widows/wives, 65, 66–67, 72
Black lung program, 8
Black population, 12
Bradley, Bill, 135
Brown, J. Douglas, 64, 69–70, 81
Burns, Eveline, 10
Business cycle, and risks, 84–85

Cardwell, James B., 102–3
Caregiver credits, 132–33
Carter administration, 113
Cates, Jerry, 45–46
Child labor, 143
Children's Bureau (1912), 143
Child support insurance, 134
Cloward, Richard, 36–37
Cohen, Wilbur, 3–4, 5–7, 17, 19, 22, 63
Commissioner, 106, 113–14

Committee on Economic Security, 4, 80
Commons, John R., 141
Complaints, 107–8
Computer technology, 103, 109
Comsumption, intertemporal distribution of, 89
Corporate planning, 129
Courts, 111–12
Coverage: expansion of, 16, 19–21, 62, 65, 69–70, 123–24; universal, 19, 21, 41, 130, 134. See also Beneficiaries; Benefits
Curtis, Carl, 34, 150

Dale, Edwin L., 124
Deficits, budget, 96
Dependency, 94, 123
Derthick, Martha, 16–17, 35–36, 46
Disability, defined, 70–72
Disability insurance program, 22, 71, 105
Disability review, 110–12, 113, 114
Dole, Robert, 56
Doughton, Robert, 73
Douglas, Paul, 81

Economic models, categories of, 87–90
Economics, 17
Economy, future of, 150–51
Education, 151–52
Eisenhower administration, 33–34
Elderly: costs of, 125; economic status of, 92; flat pension for, 23, 33–34, 41, 43; population growth of, 14; social responsibility to, 42
Employment, full, 148
Entitlement, 39, 41, 126
Epstein, Abraham, 145

Equity, 135–36; versus adequacy, 66, 130–31, 133–34

Fair Labor Standards Act (1938), 143–44
Family, size of, 94
Federal Reserve Act (1913), 143
Federal Senior Community Service Employment Program, 129
Feldstein, Martin, 83, 90, 95
Fertility, 91
Financing, 67–68, 69; failures in determining, 73; pay-as-you-go, 21, 56, 60, 63, 68, 69, 75, 84, 89, 94, 135; payroll tax, 32–33, 35, 40–42, 57, 59, 82, 85, 93, 95; public, 20; schedule, 95; temporary solutions to, 120. See also Reserves
Folsom, Marion, 65
Food stamps, 23, 132, 150
Futterman, Jack S., 101–2

Galbraith, John Kenneth, 123
General Accounting Office (GAO), 104, 107–8
Government, role of, 72–73, 105
Graebner, William, 37–38
Great Depression, 83–84, 121
Great Society, 22, 144, 145
Guaranteed annual income, 23

Haber, William, 81
Hansen, Alvin, 81
Health insurance, 21–22, 147–48, 155
Heckler, Margaret, 11
Hohaus, Reinhold, 130
House Committee on Government Operations, 103
Households, 87, 88, 90

Income, redistribution of, 35, 89
Income gap, 92

Income tax, 142–43
Individual retirement accounts
   (IRAs), 13
Inflation, 86
Institute for Poverty Research,
   134
Interest groups, 17

Johnson, Lyndon B., 144

Kean, Thomas, 20
Kennedy, John F., 16

Labor market theory, 37–38
Labor supply, 88–89, 90–91
Landon, Alfred, 59
Leadership, 45–47, 106, 113–14
Liberalism, 17, 38–39
Life-time wealth increment, 88
Linton, W. Albert, 62–63, 64–65
Litigation, 13
Longman, Philip, 125
Long-term care, 145–47, 154–55
Losing Ground (Murray), 12

McCormack, John, 123
McMahon, Theresa, 66
Marketplace, (re)entry into, 129
Markets, efficiency of, 90
Medicaid, 147, 154–55
Medicare, 145, 154, 155
Minimum wage, 143
Mortality rates, 91
Murray, Charles, 12
Murray, Philip, 63
Myers, Robert J., 3, 4–5, 8–10,
   22, 130

National Academy of Public
   Administration, 106
National Commission of Social
   Security, 101

National Commission on Social
   Security Reforms, 5
National Commission on Unem-
   ployment Compensation, 7, 149
Neoclassical synthesis, 84
New Deal, 32–33, 59
Nixon administration, 109, 113

Old-age, survivors, and disability
   insurance (OASDI), 156, 157
Old-age, survivors, disability, and
   hospital insurance (OASDHI),
   119, 124, 125, 126, 130, 133,
   136, 148, 157
Old-age and survivors insurance
   (OASI), 29, 123, 126, 153, 156
Old-age assistance, 40, 42–43, 45
Old-age insurance program: advisory panel, 81; evolution of,
   30–36, 38–45

Pay-as-you-go system, 21, 56, 60,
   63, 68, 69, 75, 84, 89, 94, 135
Payroll tax, 40–42, 57, 59; cost of,
   93; defense for, 32–33; as
   forced savings, 85; and income
   distribution, 35; and 1938 reces-
   sion, 82; regressive incidence
   of, 95
Pension: flat, 23, 33–34, 41, 43;
   private, 39, 91
Performance, 107–8
Piven, Frances, 36–37
Plan AC–12, 69–70
Plan AC–13, 71
Pluralism, 17
Policymaking, 126–28; recommen-
   dations, 128–33
Poverty, 14, 31
Pressman, Lee, 71
Private sector, 146–47
Pure Food and Drug Act, 142
Pure insurance model, 66

Race, 67, 134
Reagan, Ronald, 11–12, 15, 55, 144
Reagan administration, 110, 142
*Regulating the Poor* (Piven and Cloward), 36–37
Reserves, 67–68, 69; abandonment of, 74, 82–83; and business cycle, 64; criticism of, 58–59, 62–63; as national savings, 83; 1930s concern over, 82; potential size of, 60–61; recommendation for, 60, 72; renewed interest in, 80; retreat from, 65; surplus in, 95. *See also* Financing
Retired Senior Volunteer Program, 129
Retirement, 91; accelerated, 37; age of, 93–94; costs of, 92; decisions about, 86; from disability, 70–71; early, 89; mandatory, 128; savings for, 87
*Retirement Policies Under Social Security* (Cohen), 5
Risk, 84, 123, 127
Roosevelt, Franklin D., 4, 16, 32–32, 121
Ross, Stanford G., 102, 104–5

Savings, 85, 88, 90, 95
Self-employment, 20, 62
Self-reliance, 33
Sheppard-Towner Act (1921–1929), 143
Social adequacy, 70–71; versus equity, 66, 130–31, 133–34
Social reform, cycles of, 142–45, 153–54
Social security: and administrative capacity, 20–21; analysis models, 88; condemnation of, 58–60; confidence in, 10, 12–14;

continuities/discontinuities, 47–48; contribution of, 152; development of, 121–28; economic benefits of, 89–90; expansion of, 16, 19–21, 62, 65, 69–70, 123–24; as expression of community, 135, 136; future of, 120, 156; as implied contract, 18; insurance imagery of, 39–41, 43–45; and intergenerational tensions, 80, 92, 124–26; literature on, 30–36; macroeconomic effects of, 96; 1935 crisis in, 56; phases of, 55; policy recommendations, 128–33; and political ideology, 21; popularity of, 16–19; redefined, 48–49; as safety net, 148, 150, 151; surplus for, 14–15; as transgenerational, 6; versus welfare, 12, 13, 19–20, 44, 123
Social Security Act of 1935, 80–81; 1939 amendments to, 43, 47, 74–75, 122, 130; 1950 amendments to, 20–21, 43; 1972 amendments to, 108–9, 124; 1982 compromise, 55–56; 1983 amendments to, 120–21; singing of, 73; titles under, 122, 123, 124, 126
Social Security Administration (SSA), 4; control of, 113–14; difficulties within, 101–6; early leadership, 45–47; employee numbers, 112–13; legislative changes, 104; press coverage of, 101, 102–3, 124; reorganizations of, 103; routine vs. extraordinary tasks, 107–8
Social Security Disability Amendments of 1980 (P.L. 96–265), 110–12
Social welfare, 23–24, 31–32, 34

Special Supplemental Food Pro-
    gram for Women, Infants, and
    Children (WIC), 150
States, 105, 112, 142, 149
Stockman, David, 15, 56, 144
Supplemental Security Income
    (SSI), 8, 105, 113, 114, 131–32,
    134, 142; administrative prob-
    lems with, 109–10, 111
Svahn, John, 107

Technology, 103, 109, 150
Title I, 122, 123
Title II, 122, 123, 124, 126
Title III, 122
Title IV, 122
Title VI, 122
Title IX, 122
Title X, 122
Truman administration, 33

Unemployment, 86
Unemployment compensation, 85,
    122, 148–49, 155–56
United States Supreme Court, 112

Universal coverage, 19, 21, 41,
    130, 134
Upjohn Company, 146

Vandenberg, Arthur, 60
Vanik, Charles, 109

Wagner, Robert, 63
Weaver, Carolyn, 36, 45–46
Welfare: improvement of, 84; re-
    vision of, 149–50; and savings,
    87; versus social security, 12,
    13, 19–20, 44, 134; stigma of,
    123
Welfare Administration, 7
Welfare state, 31, 44
Williamson, W. Rulon, 4
Witte, Edwin, 5, 17, 30, 34, 62–
    63, 68, 81, 141
Women, 65, 66–67, 132
Women's Bureau (1920), 143
Workers' compensation, 18, 142
Work ethic, 40
Work programs, 129

# About the Contributors

EDWARD D. BERKOWITZ serves as an associate professor of history and director of the Program in History and Public Policy at George Washington University. He has written widely on social welfare history and policy and recently completed a study of public policy toward disability for the Twentieth Century Fund. His current research concerns the history of the Group Health Association.

MARK H. LEFF served as a Mellon fellow at Harvard University during the academic year 1985–1986. In 1986 he became an assistant professor of history at the University of Illinois. He is the author of several articles on social security and of *The Limits of Symbolic Reform* published in 1985 by Cambridge University Press.

HENRY J. AARON has written numerous books on social welfare and tax policy for the Brookings Institution. In addition to his staff position at Brookings, Aaron teaches economics at the University of Maryland and has served as Assistant Secretary of Health, Education, and Welfare for evaluation and research.

LAWRENCE H. THOMPSON directed the Office of Research and Statistics at the Social Security Administration and is currently the chief economist of the General Accounting Office. He has written many influential economic studies of social security, including an important review of the literature that appeared in the *Journal of Economic Literature.*

MARTHA DERTHICK holds a chair in the Department of Government at the University of Virginia. She previously served as director of governmental studies at Brookings, where she wrote *Uncontrollable Spending for Social Security* and *Policymaking for Social Security.*

W. ANDREW ACHENBAUM is a professor of history at Carnegie-Mellon University. He has written three important books on public policy toward the elderly, including the recently published *Social Security: Visions and Revisions.* During 1985 Achenbaum helped to arrange the Senate Special Committee on Aging's celebration of the fiftieth anniversary of social security.

WILBUR J. COHEN has been secretary of Health, Education, and Welfare, dean of the School of Education at the University of Michigan, and the Sid Richardson Professor of Public Affairs at the University of Texas. He was the Social Security Board's first employee.

ROBERT J. MYERS has served as chief actuary of the Social Security Administration and has consulted widely on social security policy with both houses of Congress and many foreign governments. Recently, he was the executive director of the National Commission on Social Security Reform.